Life is Good: Conservation in an Age of Mass Extinction

Jeremy Leon Hance

mongabay.com

mongabay.com

ISBN-13: 978-1468012507
ISBN: 1468012509

Cover photographs by Rhett Butler: beetle in Bali, Indonesia;
cheetah in Kenya; rainforest in Sumatra, Indonesia; and
deforestation in Indonesian Borneo.
Book layout and production by Rhett A. Butler

May 2012

For my wife and travel partner, Tiffany.

Environmental impact statement

Life is Good is printed on-demand, meaning books are only produced as they are ordered, which reduces excess production and waste. *Life is Good* is printed on acid-free paper stock supplied by an FSC-certified provider. In order to reduce its ecological footprint, *Life is Good* does not use glossy paper for interior pages.

At the end of each year, Mongabay.com attempts to quantify all greenhouse gas emissions associated with operations, including server and bandwidth use, travel, equipment purchases, and materials use and production. Mongabay then offsets a minimum of twice this emissions estimate by supporting an effort to conserve tropical forests in Colombia's Darien region. The initiative is run by Anthrotect, an organization that works with Afro-indigenous and Embera communities to protect forests and develop sustainable livelihoods in an area that was until recently beset by conflict and violence.

Life is Good: Conservation in an Age of Mass Extinction

Acknowledgements

To Rhett A. Butler for making all of this possible. To Tiffany Roufs, Morgan Erickson-Davis, Katie Ramos, Rhett A. Butler, William Bridges, and Carol Van Strum for editing help. To the many scientists and conservationists profiled in this book, who spend everyday working for a better world. And finally to my parents, Ed and Erva Hance, for always encouraging my love of wild things.

I thought of the long ages of the past during which the successive generations of these things of beauty [birds of paradise] had run their course. Year by year being born and living and dying amid these dark gloomy woods with no intelligent eye to gaze upon their loveliness, to all appearances such a wanton waste of beauty. It seems sad that on the one hand such exquisite creatures should live out their lives and exhibit their charms only in these wild inhospitable regions. This consideration must surely tell us that all living things were not made for man, many of them have no relation to him, their happiness and enjoyment's, their loves and hates, their struggles for existence, their vigorous life and early death, would seem to be immediately related to their own well-being and perpetuation alone.

—The Malay Archipelago, Alfred Russel Wallace

Introduction: the life emergency

Life is good. One doesn't have to be a philosopher, a moralist, a theologian, or even a scientist to know this is so: from algae to elephants and boas to oaks, life is good. In fact, it's not humanity that makes Earth unique as it swings around the sun; instead it's life—varied, innumerable, collective life—that makes our blue planet stand out amid the vastness of space.

Of course, as Homo sapiens we can only view the bustling life around us through our senses, hampered as they are by our limitations. With our, at times, bizarre love of hierarchy we have signaled out some species as more beautiful than others and some as more useful; there are those we fear and loathe and a few we call our own. But the truth is that life in all its fullness and diversity is what is good.

The blue arrow poison frog seeking shade in the leaf litter is good. The cheetah suffocating the antelope with a throat-bite is good. The earthstar fungus sending out spores amid a rain shower is good. The wandering albatross casting its shadow on the far-flung waves is good. The red-eyed cicada singing metallically on a eucalyptus tree is good. The school of slender rainbow sardines twisting en masse in the cold seawater is good. The scarab beetle rolling its Sisyphean dung boulder across the wide dunes is good. The plankton floating down through the lightless dark to the abyssal plain is good. The yew standing through the ages in a rolling country graveyard is good. The white-winged nightjar sleeping in the long grass is good.

Now in a bizarre twist of natural history, the survival of all these is dependent on one bipedal, big-brained organism: us.

Forecast: mass extinction

Our past does not always speak well for us.

On July 3rd, 1888, three men killed the last of the great auks (*Pinguinus impennis*). A nesting pair were found on the island of Eldey; they were strangled by two of the men, while the third man stepped on the last great auk egg, crushing it beneath his boot. This unique bird—the penguin of the northern hemisphere—may have once numbered in the millions, surviving hundreds of thousands of years being preyed on by small human communities. However, decades of overexploitation for food and feathers—used in pillows—as well as wealthy Europeans collecting great auk eggs as decorations ultimately resulted in the marine bird's obliteration.

Much like penguins, the great auk was awkward and ungainly on land, but a dancer in the water. They fed on fish and other small marine species. During breeding season they reproduced in massive colonies, thus becoming easy prey for hunters and egg-collectors. Though they bred largely on remote, sometimes barely-accessible islands, this did not save them.

The story of the great auk, however, is unique. Most species go extinct in the dark like a dog who retreats into the woods to breathe its last with quiet dignity. While these endings may still be the product of human impacts, they occur far beyond human eyes, and may take us many years, often decades, to confirm. For the great auk, unusually, we have the date and place of its undeserved demise.

The great auk is not alone. Such extinctions—seen and unseen—are piling up. In much of the past, big extinctions were relatively rare events. For the most part, species are robust and hardy, capable of surviving a number of changes to their respective environments, often withstanding more than we might expect. However, five times in the past half billion years species have vanished with sudden ferocity—including whole types of animals such as dinosaurs, mosasaurs and plesiosaurs (great sea monsters), eurypterids (giant marine arthropods), ammonites (octopi-like marine invertebrates), blastoids (sea buds), trilobites (marine anthropods), therapsids (reptiles that gave rise to mammals), and archosaurs (which gave rise to crocodiles and birds). It's almost as though entire evolutionary paths were suddenly discarded in a fiery furnace. During these life conflagrations 50-90 percent of species vanished. When the dust settled, evolution started anew and those still around repopulated the world, creating new forms from old survivors. But millions and millions of years would have to pass before species-diversity returned to past-levels.

This is the situation the world currently faces. Scientists have been warning for decades that the Earth is headed toward another mass extinction. If it occurs, or is occurring even as I write (as many fear), it would be the sixth since life rose out of the sea. But it would be the only one caused by a single species.

Each of the past mass extinctions was coupled with vast global changes that drastically changed the planet, often upsetting the dominant big species and overturning old ecological hierarchies. In the case of the current extinction, that would be mammals, maybe birds, and perhaps most importantly the incredibly brief tyranny of humans. A mass extinction will irrevocably interrupt the environments that we—as humans—depend on, in spite of our technology, our swagger, and our self-imposed alienation from nature.

Since our evolutionary rise in East Africa 200,000 years ago, we have changed the world in a geographic blink of an eye: from harnessing fire to cutting down forests, from plowing grasslands to mining mountain tops, from damming rivers to drilling up the hydrocarbons from billions of life forms for crude energy. Today, most species are imperiled by habitat loss, deforestation, pollution, overexploitation for food and medicine, invasive species, and, since the industrial age, climate change. This multitude of factors occurring synergistically—and propelled by a steadily rising human population consuming ever-more resources—has pushed a vast number of species to the brink, and hundreds, that we know of, to extinction already.

Scientists estimate that species are vanishing somewhere between 100 and 1,000 times the background rate, i.e. the average rate determined by the fossil record. For example, the fossil record shows that on average two mammals go extinct every million years, but in the last 500 years at least 80 mammals have been pushed to extinction: mammals like the thylacine (*Thylacinus cynocephalus*), the Caribbean monk seal (Monachus tropicalis), and within the last decade the Yangtze River dolphin (*Lipotes vexillifer*). During most of history, extinctions are balanced out by the evolution of new species; now, however, extinctions are well outpacing evolution. Overall, since 1500 AD—just after Columbus reached the New World—the International Union for the Conservation of Nature (IUCN) has documented 875 extinctions.

This number, as alarming as it is, is a vast underestimate. Many species probably vanished before ever being documented by science, since the systematic cataloguing of life on Earth only began in the 18th Century and has progressed slowly since then (at least compared to the number of species on Earth). Other species have not been seen for decades—in some cases more than a century—but have yet to be declared extinct, since no one has yet ventured to their forgotten homes to have a look. Confirmation of extinction is not an easy or cheap endeavor, so their status waits on intrepid researchers, and a lack of funds and resources means many species have been waiting a long, long time.

Scientists have catalogued further evidence of a current mass extinction beyond documented extinctions and estimates: the number of species endangered worldwide. The IUCN's Red List, which deals with such issues, has worked tirelessly for more than a decade to answer just this question. Currently the Red List has evaluated just over 45,000 species. Of these 22 percent are currently considered threatened with extinction, and if the Near Threatened category is added the percentage jumps to 29. In addition, nearly 8,000 species are considered Data Deficient, meaning researchers simply don't have enough information to determine the species' status one way or another. So, the actual percentage may well be up to a third.

Some types of species are faring worse than others according to the Red List. While mammals and reptiles are close to the average (25 and 22 percent respectively), amphibians face a dire emergency. In combination with the other environmental impacts hitting all species families, amphibians are also fighting a fatal fungal disease. To date, 41 percent of amphibians are listed as threatened. In fact, it looks as though amphibians may be the first widespread victims of the current mass extinction crisis, perhaps even going the way of the dinosaurs.

At the other end of the spectrum, birds may be faring the best of all: 13 percent of the world's birds are imperiled. While they are doing better than most, it's not exactly cause for celebration or passivity: to put it in other terms 'only' 1,300 birds are currently facing extinction, which is several hundred more species than the number of birds found in all of North America, migrants included.

However, for many types of life we simply don't know how imperiled they are. Of the species described and named by researchers, the IUCN Red List has only evaluated 2.3 percent, leaving out most reptiles, fish, fungi, plants, and invertebrates (which make up the bulk of life on Earth) both on land and in the sea.

Scientists' predictions of mass extinction began on the land. In the later 20th Century, researchers saw how much terrestrial habitat was being lost worldwide, especially due to the on-going destruction of the world's rainforests, and began to calculate— and at times to bicker over—the extent of the current life crisis. By 1998, however, a poll of 400 biologists found that 70 percent of the scientists believed there was enough evidence to say a mass extinction was underway, and that percentage is growing. A survey in 2011 found that 99.5 percent of nearly 600 conservation scientists agreed a significant biodiversity loss was "likely" to "virtually certain." Still, until recently, the focus has been solely on terrestrial species. Now it has become increasingly clear that human impacts are changing the ocean's biodiversity just as much as the land's.

A recent panel of experts convened by the International Program on the State of the Ocean (IPSO) reported that we have so altered the oceans that mass extinction is becoming a reality: overfishing, pollution, and climate change are impacting marine ecosystems in ways not seen during human history. There is now no environment one could deem safe.

Conservation as an answer

To the perils of mass extinction, human kind has put forward an answer: conservation. Conservation is any activity that works to preserve species and ecosystems from destruction, including establishing protected areas, passing new legislation, rearing endangered species in captivity, restoring damaged ecosystems, and the broad education of the public, among other efforts. While conservation efforts took off in the 19th Century, they really didn't go global until the 20th Century.

To date, conservationists' greatest success is arguably the vast network of protected areas worldwide. Currently there are more than 100,000 protected areas, covering around 13 percent of the world's land surface. However, not all protected areas are created equal: some have opened their doors to industrial activities, such as oil extraction and logging. In fact, fewer than half the total protected areas are delineated as under "strict protection." Even strictly protected areas are often marred by illegal logging, poaching, a lack of funding, and a paucity of rangers. Finally, protected areas have often been established without biodiversity's broader needs in mind; most of the world's great migrations are now cut off and many species are trapped in protected areas, unable to disseminate elsewhere, making them vulnerable, for even the best protected area in the world can't keep out climate change or disease. While on land protected areas have spread worldwide, the process has been far slower in the oceans: today just over 1 percent of the ocean is under protection.

Still, even with their imperfections, conservationists view protected areas as essential to saving the world's species. In 2010 the UN's Convention on Biological Diversity (CBD)—which includes 193 member nations (though notably not the U.S.)—pledged to expand protected areas to 17 percent of land and 10 percent of the sea by 2020.

Beyond the establishment of protected areas, conservation efforts have also focused on changing local and national laws to protect species with notable, though often uneven, success worldwide. When utilized the U.S. Endangered Species Act has saved dozens of species from extinction, though many have vanished while lingering on its Kafkaesque "candidate list." The global Convention on International Trade in Endangered Species of Wild Fauna and Flora (CITES) has protected hundreds of species from overexploitation by outright banning trade or making regulations. Currently around 800 species are banned from global trade. A final example is Costa Rica's Biodiversity Law, which won the CBD's Future Policy 2010 award and has helped the nation become known as one of the 'greenest' in the world and among the 'happiest'. The law focuses on conservation, sustainable use, and providing benefits to many stakeholders including locals and indigenous people. Many nations have good biodiversity laws on the dockets, which they are simply ignored by law enforcement and courts.

Conservation efforts have also targeted certain species, often focusing on the big and the charismatic. In many cases, such efforts have not been in vain: the white rhino (*Ceratotherium simum*) fell to just around 100 individuals but today numbers 17,500, making this species the most populous of the world's rhinos; the American bison's (*Bison bison*) story is similar with around 30,000 wild bison surviving today after a close brush with oblivion; the bald eagle (*Haliaeetus leucocephalus*) has also recovered in the U.S. after legal protection and the banning of the pesticide, DDT; the Arabian oryx (*Eschrichtius robustus*) has gone from extinct in the wild to 1,000 wild individuals due to breeding and reintroductions by zoos; reintroductions have also boosted golden lion tamarins (*Leontopithecus rosalia*) in Brazil's Atlantic Forest; the world's last representative of a wild horse, Przewalksi's horse (*Equus ferus przewalskii*), has gone from a population nadir of 12 to around 1,400 horses, including both captive and wild; the humpback whale (*Megaptera novaeangliae*) has bounced back from 1,500 animals to around 80,000 today, due wholly to a landmark ban on whaling, which saved many other cetacean species from imminent extinction.

Working in conservation, though, is playing the long game. A number of beloved species have seen incredibly devoted conservation work, but their long-term survival remains in doubt, such as tigers, gorillas, chimpanzees, and orangutans, as well as the world's elephant and rhino species. Most threatened species, however, are not these. They are instead the multitude of insects, plants, and fungi that have never seen targeted conservation efforts and either linger on or vanish in obscurity.

While conservation has achieved much in the last century, the movement has nowhere succeeded in its ultimate goal: stemming the loss of global biodiversity and the large-scale destruction of ecosystems. Conservation remains a David-vs.-Goliath battle, and Goliath gets bigger with every year.

To stay effective and relevant, conservation is asking new questions and changing with the times. The following 14 essays in this book are a scattershot of just a few of the recent changes in conservation: from new tools (camera traps and genetics) to new ideas (shifting baselines and conservation language); from questioning old models ('trickle down conservation' and entertainment zoos) to highlighting long-ignored species (the solenodon and the Bornean rhino); and from big emergencies (the oceans and migrations) to new research (top predators and jellyfish).

But does it matter?

One of the great evolutionary wonders of Homo sapiens sapiens is our ability to adapt to any new situation with extreme rapidity. Drop us into Antarctica and we will not waste much time in mental shock, but will do our best, which is to say our cleverest, to survive. While this adaptability is one of the key reasons for our survival, there is a downside: we have a tendency to mentally adapt quite quickly to our changing world with little protest. Our personal, and even cultural, memory quickly forgets what is no longer there. Who thinks about what salmon runs were like in North America before rivers were dammed? Who can remember when the Tasmanian wolf—now long extinct—was considered a nuisance? Who can recall the seas rife with whales before commercial whaling? Who remembers New York City when it was deciduous forest? Biodiversity, absent, is largely forgotten.

So why does it matter? Why should we care if one-third, a half, or three-quarters of the world's species vanish in the next few centuries? Over 90 percent of species that have ever lived are now extinct, so why should today's species matter?

From a simply human perspective the answer is quite easy: it's about us.

Extinctions don't occur in a vacuum; they have rippling effects outward through the ecosystem. Sometimes another species may pick up some of the ecological slack left behind by an untimely demise, but that's not always the case. More often the loss of one species dooms another, as they are deeply interconnected: pollinator and flower, predator and prey, seed disperser and tree. Although no one knows where the critical tipping point lies, eventually the loss of too many species means a collapse in the ecosystem. And, for all our bluster, we depend on the environment for survival.

Biodiversity, the richness of life on Earth, provides a number of services to humanity such as pollination, pest control, medicinal discoveries, food production, fisheries, carbon sequestration, clean freshwater, soil health, and, of course, the immeasurable value of sharing the world with a wide variety of weird and wonderful life-forms. It's safe to predict that if the Earth suffers another mass extinction, most ecosystems would falter and collapse, and, make no mistake, human society as we know it—and enjoy it—would very likely follow.

Hypothetically, let's say we did survive a global mass extinction, how would we thrive? Without the variety and immensity of life on Earth, our art, our philosophies, our religions would pale and diminish. Beauty would be trodden over. Curiosity would lag. Not only would we suffer physically from environmental degradation, we would suffer spiritually from a lonely, less interesting, and less beautiful world. Zoos, assuming civilization still plodded along, would become mass totems to a lost and better world. And the generations that caused this upheaval—through a lack of wisdom and foresight—would rightly be cursed by those to come. Who would forgive those who stamped out the wonder of life on Earth?

On July 3rd, 1888, three men brutally killed the last of the great auks. A hundred and twenty three years later, we may regard the actions of these men as untenable and barbaric. But our generations are already implicated in far worse: the destruction of the world's forests, the plunder of the global oceans, and the changing of our climate.

Still there is time and hope: mass extinction has not occurred yet and the challenges to the world's ecosystems are solvable. The solutions are there; it's the will that has been lacking. Life on Earth has a chance, if we choose to give it one.

1

Meeting Tam in Borneo: our last chance to save the world's smallest rhino

Nothing can really prepare a person for coming face-to-face with what may be the last of a species.

I had known for a week that I would be fortunate enough to meet Tam. I'd heard stories of his gentle demeanor, discussed his current situation with experts, and read everything I could find about this surprising individual. But still, walking up to the pen where Tam stood contentedly pulling leaves from the hands of a local ranger, hearing him snort and whistle, watching as he rattled the bars with his blunted horn, I felt like I was walking into a place I wasn't meant to be. As though

I was treading on his, Tam's, space: entering into a cool deep forest where mud wallows and shadows still linger. This was Tam's world, or at least it should've been.

A living—still surviving—Bornean rhinoceros, Tam is one of an estimated forty left in the world, maybe fewer. At 620 kilograms (1430 pounds), Tam is a full-grown male. Researchers have estimated his age to be about twenty with at least another decade before him. Surprisingly pinkish in color, he is sparsely covered by large black hairs, while both of his two horns—unlike other Asian rhinos which only sport one—have been rubbed dull against the walls of his pen.

Tam is a survivor—that is certain. He survived his forest habitat being whittled into smaller and smaller pockets. He survived his right foot being caught in a poacher's snare, leaving an inch-wide white scar circling his ankle. And he survived wandering directly into an oil palm plantation in early August of last year, probably propelled by his injury. He had beaten the odds, this one.

Everything has changed for Tam now.

Cynthia Ong, the director of Land Empowerment Animals and People (LEAP)—an organization that has worked on raising funds to save the Bornean rhino—told me that since Tam had wandered into a plantation over a year ago, the three-quarter-ton rhino had become "very manja". Not being Malaysian I didn't know the word, but she assured me every Malaysian mother's daughter knew it, and it meant something like 'lovingly spoiled'.

It's true that Tam has entered a kind of retirement. Instead of being butchered for his horn—a fate suffered by a female Bornean rhino in 2001—Tam was immediately seen as a symbol of a dying, but not yet dead, species. His surprising arrival on an oil palm plantation brought the government and conservation community of Sabah into action. He now has a 2.5 hectare pen to his own, complete with forest cover and two mud wallows; he is fed a selection of greens gathered every morning and afternoon by rangers with the Sabah Wildlife Department; and he is protected 24-7 by an armed anti-poaching squad.

Of course, the situation is not perfect. It would have been best if Tam could have remained in the wild to live out his life—only this time near other rhinos, instead of the forest patch where he was trapped and alone. But his injured foot had required care and now he is too accustomed to humans to be placed back in the wild, because he would likely wander into human habitations again—where he may not be so lucky.

However his appearance on the human stage has given Tam another role to play: a survivor's role.

Tam—this massive, purplish, very 'manja' animal who almost crushed my hand against the bars as I tried to take rapid photos into his pen, because he probably thought I was trying to feed him the camera—could be the key to bringing the Bornean rhino back from the brink.

The story of the two-horned Asian rhino

The story of Tam and his kind goes back—way back.

Bornean rhinos are actually a subspecies of the Sumatran rhino, of which there are only an estimated 250 left in the world. Sumatran rhinos—and their Bornean subspecies—are the last remaining rhinos in the genus *Dicerorhinus*. Most researchers believe that the Sumatran rhino is the last living representative of early Miocene rhinos and therefore the oldest rhino species left in the world, one that emerged between 15 and 20 million years ago. For those keeping track, that's over 10 million years before the ancestors of humans split from chimpanzees.

This also makes the Sumatran rhino the closest living relative to the legendary woolly rhinoceros, which roamed the steppes during the Ice Age. Evidence of their ancient ancestry is seen in the Sumatran rhinos' thick black strands of hair, the same hair that probably covered the woolly rhinoceros, only in a far thicker coat.

For millions of years the Sumatran rhino inhabited Southeast Asia, from Borneo to Northeastern India. Living largely solitary lives, they preferred deep tropical forests near muddy and swampy areas. Not known to fight over territory, the Sumatran rhino is actually quite a gentle creature, despite its heavy bulk and huge horns. Considered the most vocal of all the rhinos, it makes a number of surprising noises, including ones that have been compared to whales singing.

After millions of years, the rhino's fate turned. Following the path similar to many lost and threatened species in the region, habitat destruction and large-scale hunting drove the rhino into smaller and smaller pockets until it finally reached its current pathetic state. The rhino's horn is key to understanding the demise of the animal; it fetches more than gold or cocaine (upwards of $50,000 per kilo) on the black market where it is sold as traditional Chinese medicine. Despite decades of anti-poaching measures and laws, the trade—buttressed by well-financed and connected underground criminal syndicates—is still booming, and rhinos across the world are still paying the price. In fact, the past few years have seen poaching hit record highs. Yet science has shown repeatedly that rhino horn has the same curative benefits as eating one's hair or fingernails, in other words none.

The Sumatran rhino has already lost one subspecies to extinction—the Northern Sumatran rhino, once prevalent in India, Burma, and Bangladesh—while the remaining two subspecies—the Bornean and the Western Sumatran rhino—hang on by a thread in Borneo, Sumatra, and perhaps peninsular Malaysia.

On top of all of this, Junaidi Payne, chairman of the Borneo Rhinoceros Alliance (BORA) and longtime conservationist with WWF (World Wide Fund for Nature)-Malaysia, says that a new and insidious threat faces the species: population collapse.

"Death rate eventually exceeds birth rate, even with adequate habitat and zero poaching," Payne says. "Poaching will hasten the extinction of the Sumatran rhino, but is no longer the main driver of its extinction."

Habitat is so fragmented and rhino numbers so low, that many remaining animals are simply unable to locate another individual to breed with. They are caught in pockets of forest surrounded by oil palm plantations with no opportunity to safely cross the plantations and reach other rhinos. Tam is an example of this: his front foreleg was caught in a snare that was mostly likely put out by plantation workers.

"Most workers in oil palm plantations, as well as rural people in general, do not earn big incomes and survive how they can," says Payne. Palm oil plantation workers—mostly immigrants from Indonesia and the Philippines in Sabah—as well as locals in some areas, are known to set snares to catch deer and other animals for meat, but these snares trap indiscriminately and sometimes injure or kill Bornean rhinos, sun bears, elephants, and other imperiled species.

But it's not just the situation on the ground that has brought the Sumatran rhino so close to extinction; it is also a matter of perception. During a discussion in Cynthia Ong's Kota Kinabalu home, Payne and Ong told me that Tam and his kind have been largely overlooked by the public, both locally and internationally.

"People don't understand the significance of the rhino," Ong says, who describes the Sumatran rhino as "one of the top five endangered mammals in the world." Ong, a native of Sabah who lived in California for a number of years before returning, adds that Sabahians simply don't realize how rare the Sumatran rhino is or its evolutionary importance as the last representative of an ancient mammal line.

Here, most of the focus is on orangutans with elephants coming a distant second. When compared to the huge amount of information available on orangutans, there are few research papers or books, and no documentary films, on Sumatran rhinos. Any conservationist knows that it is difficult to save a species that doesn't excite the imagination of the public—or garner the funds needed for conservation efforts—and since these rhinos are so secretive and rare they have largely been out of sight, out of mind.

"It could be an intimate relationship [between humans and rhinos], but how we choose to engage shows us where we are at as a human community," Ong says.

The good news is that the Sumatran rhino has a new champion. Having worked to save numerous species in Sabah, Junaidi

Payne says that he has now dedicated the rest of his life to saving the embattled rhino.

However, his decision raises some eyebrows.

Why work to save a doomed species?

Why? Junaidi Payne gets asked this question all the time. Why work to save a species that is doomed to extinction? Why not work on a species with a little more promise (not to mention better potential for fundraising), like, say, the orangutan or elephant?

"Simple reason," Payne told me. "There are estimated to be 11,000 orangutans [in Sabah alone] and probably 1,500 [Bornean pygmy] elephants, but there are no more than forty rhinos and new populations have stagnated and are going down slowly. It's about need."

However, Payne is not shy about the difficulties facing him and others who have joined the new effort to save the Bornean rhino.

With perhaps only 2-3 fertile female Bornean rhinos left in existence he says, "anyone, any common sense person, would agree that [attempting to save the subspecies] is a waste of time."

I asked Payne if he believed then that the rhino was doomed.

"Probably," he answered, "yet maybe not." And it is that 'maybe not' that really interests and excites Payne. He remains hopeful—and perhaps with good reason.

Payne pointed out to me that past conservation success stories prove the rhino is not a lost cause. At the end of the nineteenth century, Africa's white rhinoceros—once widespread—were down to just over twenty individuals surviving in one location in South Africa. Intensive conservation measures pulled the white rhino back from the brink: today an estimated 17,480 white rhinos live in east and southern Africa, making it the most populous rhino species on the planet.

But it's not just the white rhino: over one thousand European bison survive today, all of which are descended from just a dozen individuals in captivity; in three years captive breeding has brought the Caribbean's blue iguana from 25 individuals to 500; and after going extinct in the wild in the 1970s, over a thousand Arabian oryx have been successfully reintroduced into their native habitat.

Despite these and other success stories, Payne says that there has been a "strange change where academics claim [species] are doomed unless you have a certain minimum number of individuals—often the number 500 has been proposed."

Payne calls this "the geneticist's tyranny" where in spite of "empirical evidence" that large mammals have gone through genetic bottlenecks and come back, many geneticists would claim that the fate of the rhino is already decided.

"People are forced to give reasons why we save these species," Ong added, but it's clear that "you can change the course of events."

Of course, the question of "why?" could be asked of any endangered animal. Why put money, time, and energy into saving a species at all? Certainly, species provide what are called "ecosystem services"; acting in concert with their environment, they give us pollination, clean water, clean air, food, medicine etc. But are there other reasons?

"I can only say—I'm shy to say it [...] but the general answer would be that humans, having even thought about [saving a species], gives some responsibility to actually save them," Payne said.

This was an illuminating statement by Payne, given that in the course of conversation he relentlessly stuck to the facts: what could be known scientifically. During my time in Sabah, I learned that Payne, a British citizen who has adopted the state of Sabah for his own, was capable of dispelling bullshit with a glance. At times this characteristic may make him appear prickly, but it also gives him a focus and a realism lacking in many conservationists.

Ong, on the other hand, largely provided the emotive, spiritual, and moral reasons behind their work. In fact, she spoke of Tam like a newly discovered ancestor in a voice that sometimes seemed to sing with enthusiasm. They were the pair: but despite their obvious differences, they never clashed, only complemented one another. I wondered if their differing strengths together could be the key to saving the animal.

Not surprisingly, Ong agreed with Payne that the decision to save a species says just as much about humans as it does about the embattled and vanishing species: "I see this as a question of where we are in our evolution and how do we respond to this critical situation."

She then puts it in more personal term: "When our great grandchildren ask 'when you found out about [the rhino] what did you do?' how will we respond?"

The plan going forward

Of course, it's not enough to simply decide to save a species on the precipice of extinction; action requires long-term commitment, perseverance, and, let's not be shy, a lot of money. In the case of Sumatran rhinos, there has already been a concerted effort to save the species—which ended in failure.

In 1984 the IUCN brought together a wide range of interested parties from Peninsular Malaysia, Sabah, Indonesia, the United States, and Britain to discuss how to save the Sumatran rhino. They decided the best thing would be a globally managed program of captured individuals for breeding in captivity in a number of different locations. Between 1986 to1994, around forty Sumatrans rhinos, including some Bornean rhinos, were caught and placed in zoos, as well as other closely managed situations.

The government of Sabah embraced the plan. In 1988 they established Sabah Wildlife Department, previously a division of the Forestry Department, which was created in part as a means to facilitate rhino conservation.

Unfortunately the well-thought-out plan didn't produce: only one breeding pair was successfully established in the Cincinnati Zoo, bearing three offspring. Nearly all the original rhinos caught are now dead; the only female to bear offspring died in 2009.

Payne says this initiative failed due to 'pure bad luck' but also "to some doses of politics, ego, and people with opinions, whose opinions unfortunately were wrong."

Starting in the late 1990s, another breeding site of 100 hectares was established at Way Kambas on Sumatra. However, while the conservation center includes three females and two males, no offspring have been born. Unfortunately a pregnancy in 2010 was lost. Conservationists hope success will come soon, as it's common for a female rhino to lose a first pregnancy. But Payne isn't holding his breath.

"The thinking is that the whole idea of very closely managed rhinos in captivity isn't working as well or as fast as is needed to save the species," Payne says.

In 2007 researchers concluded at a Conference on Rhino Conservation in Sabah that due to reproductive issues and possible inbreeding, rhino numbers in the Malaysian state had stagnated and were probably declining, therefore simply preserving habitat for rhinos would not save them, nor they thought would captivity. A bold and innovative proposal was put forth.

As Payne tells it, the conservation community was confronted with a choice: either do nothing or place rhinos in a large conservation area that would be less closely managed.

Now, Payne and BORA are in the midst of assisting the Sabah Wildlife Department in implementing a vast fenced-in sanctuary—4,500 hectares—where Bornean rhinos can be brought together. The rhinos will be monitored, but will have "minimal human influences". They will be largely left alone in the hopes that nature will take its course and the rhinos will breed.

"In theory we are putting one half of Sabah's rhino eggs in one basket," Payne says of the plan.

"In semi-natural fenced conditions, the close monitoring [...] potentially allows things to be done that would be impossible in the wild. This might include providing better nutrition or administering hormones to boost reproductive prospects," he explains. Payne believes it may be necessary at some point to bring in as many rhinos as can be found.

Ong adds that conservationists have to "make a decision to go all the way with human intervention or why bother?"

Only rhinos that are cut off from others will be placed in the new sanctuary. If rhinos in parks like Tabin or Danum are determined to still be breeding on their own, they will not be a part of the sanctuary, but will be left in the wild and staunchly protected by anti-poaching units.

The proto-sanctuary already has its first two residents. One is, of course, none other than Tam, who is biding his time until the new sanctuary is built. The other, brought in after my visit, is an old female named Gelogob who had been kept at the Kota Kinabulu zoo. Unfortunately, she is too old to mate. However, another younger female has been located and the team is currently attempting to trap her for transport. If all goes according to plan Tam will soon come face-to-face with a viable mate, perhaps his first ever.

Payne says that the sanctuary only needs one more male and another female to make the program "just about doable".

The plan has received full support from the government and funds have been promised to the tune of 8 million ringgits by the national government (over $2 million) and 250,000 ringgits ($70,000) by the State Ministry of Tourism, Culture and Environment for interim holding paddocks for rhinos. The sanctuary has also received a large donation by the Sime Darby Foundation, a corporate social and environmental responsibility arm of one of Malaysia's largest palm oil companies.

"Director of Sabah Forestry Department, Datuk Sam Mannan, and Sabah Minister of Tourism, Culture and Environment, Datuk Masidi Manjun have both taken lead roles in supporting the early stages of the program, and both have shown a strong personal interest in pushing it forward," says Payne.

Masidi, well-known in Sabah for his unwavering commitment to environmental issues, headlined a fundraiser in the spring organized by LEAP that raised 530,000 ringgits ($150,000) for BORA. Without such government support, the plan to save the rhinos would have stalled before it even started. Still, Payne and others say that investments of private money are very much needed.

All that needs to happen now is implementation on the ground and securing a few more rhinos; however the construction of the center has been moving slowly. Too slowly for Payne.

"As one gets older, time seems to go quickly. Even allowing for that, I am quite frustrated with the slow speed of progress in construction of the long-term Borneo Rhino Sanctuary," he says. The waiting and bureaucracy have become almost unbearable.

"This is what happens when a species is close to the end, and we procrastinate, and muddle along guided by committees and caution," he adds.

Even with setbacks, Payne believes that Sabah is the best hope for Sumatran rhino conservation, despite Indonesia having a larger population of rhinos.

"Due to human population pressures in Indonesia and the massive expansion of big-scale plantations that compete for land with small-holders," Payne says that "it may be only a matter of time before the Sumatran rhino vanishes from the wild in Indonesia."

A large number of unanswered questions remain—such as just how many rhinos are left and how many are capable of breeding—but Payne says that answers to these questions are largely unnecessary for conservation efforts.

"What is the point spending 10 years researching if the population is 10 or 15 individuals when the species is still going down?" he asked.

Conservation, according to Payne, cannot always wait for hard science and data; often it comes down to using one's "best judgment" at the time to save a species.

And if the worst happens: if no other rhinos are caught, or other rhinos are caught but mating never results in offspring, and the species slips away into the jungle night, conservationists do have a last-ditch, desperate plan that relies on future technology: bring the species back from the dead.

Researchers with the Leibniz Institute for Zoo and Wildlife Research are attempting to use hormones to extract viable eggs from Gelogob, the aging female. If eggs are obtained they will be frozen in liquid nitrogen for the future.

"It is very likely that further advances in large mammal reproductive technology will mean that embryos could be fostered in the womb of other rhino species," explains Payne. However, two attempts so far have failed to deliver viable eggs for freezing. A third and likely final attempt is planned.

But conservationists hope it doesn't come to bringing the species back from the grave.

Tam, again

When I left Tam the first time, I thought it would be the last. But the next morning, to my surprise, we were able to visit him again. Beforehand, we followed rangers with the Sabah Wildlife Department in a pickup as they cut branches, leaves, and vines for Tam's breakfast.

By the time we reached Tam, he was already waiting at the gate where they feed him, rubbing his head against the bars. Tam was "like a cat rubbing against you", Cynthia Ong had told me, and it was true. He would rub his head along the bars like a pet asking for attention. In fact, he had largely rubbed away his magnificent horn. This shouldn't be seen as a bad thing: without a horn he is of less interest to poachers.

Ong described the day that Tam wandered injured into the palm oil plantation as a "fortuitous and unplanned event", because "it pushed the idea of [the] proposal" to start a massive rhino sanctuary.

Tam, she told me, "is not an accident".

After eating his breakfast—carefully measured out on a scale meant for a giant—and having his photo taken a few hundred times, Tam turned and made his way back into the forest. First, he spent a moment wading in the mud and then slowly, but surely, he wandered back into the deep green of Borneo's jungle. One moment he was there, roaming on the forest's edge, and the next he was gone as if he had never been.

Days before, when I asked Junaidi Payne if this was the last chance to save the species, he told me simply: "Yes."

It's true that this story will end in one of two ways. In the first, Tam and all of his kind will vanish from the dwindled forest, leaving not even their ghosts behind. In this version, he will become another member of those animals painted so nicely in books on extinction: Tam, I imagine, will appear somewhere between the dodo, the thylacine, and the moa.

In the second version, Tam and his kind will continue inhabiting the deep, largely unseen areas of Southeast Asia's magnificent forests. While this version is dependent on many factors not in our control—factors where previous generations have already failed the rhino—it is our choice now whether or not we give this ending a chance.

I don't know what we will find when the last page is turned, but having been among the fortunate few to come face-to-face with the two-horned rhino of Asia, I can't help but dread the day we fail, while simultaneously hoping for the day where I can take my children to meet Tam's.

2

Will jellyfish take over the world?

It could be a plot of a (bad) science-fiction film: a man-made disaster spawns millions upon millions of jellyfish, which rapidly take over the ocean. Humans, starving for mahi-mahi and Chilean sea bass, turn to jellyfish, which becomes the new tuna (after the tuna fishery has collapsed, of course). Fish sticks become jelly-sticks, fish-and-chips become jelly-and-chips, and California rolls become jellyrolls. The sci-fi film could end with the ominous image of a jellyfish evolving air-breathing pumps and pulling itself onto land with barbed tentacles—readying itself for a new conquest.

While this scenario sounds ridiculous, all of it—except the last sentence, of course—could conceivably come to pass if humanity continues to ignore the diminishing health of the oceans, say scientists. Anthony Richardson and colleagues call this the 'jellyfish joyride' and it is already happening in parts of the ocean: diverse fish populations are being replaced by gelatinous aggregations.

"Dense jellyfish blooms are a natural feature of healthy ocean ecosystems, but a clear picture is now emerging of more severe and frequent jellyfish outbreaks worldwide," Richardson, from the University of Queensland and CSIRO Climate Adaptation Flagship, explains. "In recent years, jellyfish blooms have been recorded in the Mediterranean, the Gulf of Mexico, the Black and Caspian Seas, off the Northeast U.S. coast, Southern Africa, and particularly in Far East coastal waters."

Once jellyfish gain a foothold, Richardson says they can establish a massive population at the expense of other ocean life assuming conditions are right: "the problem is that jellyfish might form an alternative 'stable state.' What this means is that parts of the ocean might switch from being dominated by fish to being dominated by jellyfish."

Few animals in the world are more bizarre than the jellyfish. Lacking a backbone, jellyfish have actually no relation to fish—despite their common name—instead they belong to a phylum, Cndaria, which includes corals, sea anemones, and hydroids. All members of Cndaria share a similar body type of a tube that is closed on one end and open on the other. In general, the jellyfish's tube body resembles a bell, a light bulb, an umbrella or any other perfectly symmetrical tapered orb one can imagine. The term "jelly" comes from the fact that these creatures' bodies are made up of two thin cell walls with a kind of gelatinous substance in between, known as a "mesoglea."

Jellyfish do not have brains proper or a central nervous system; instead a diffuse network of nerves compiles what researchers have dubbed a "nerve net." Much of our understanding of how these free-floating neurons work is limited.

A well-known aspect of jellyfish is their tentacles, which have given some of their kind the biological name of Medusae, after the Greek diva with snakes for hair. Long strand-like limbs, the tentacles are the part of the jellyfish that, depending on the species, may be poisonous and even deadly to swimmers and beachcombers.

So, we have a thin-skinned gelatinous organism—not unlike a stuffed crepe—with tentacles that react to stimuli with a map of nerves. This shouldn't make us underestimate them: jellyfish are incredibly successful organisms. With over 2,000 known species, they are ridiculously diverse: some are only an inch long while others spread over 100 feet; some glow in the dark while others are translucent, and many are hypnotically beautiful. In truth, jellyfish have been around at least 500 million years, which perhaps makes us—not them—the odd ones out. But their sudden dominance in parts of the ocean could spell a drastic depletion of marine biodiversity.

In a 2009 study appearing in Trends in Ecology and Evolution, Richardson and colleagues explore the causes behind the jellyfish infestation and the need for swift, decisive action to stem the jellyfish take-over. Jellyfish explosions are linked directly to human actions, including over-fishing, the input of fertilizer and sewage into the ocean, and climate change.

Overfishing has removed fish from marine ecosystems at astounding rates. According to Richardson this has opened the door for jellyfish to take their place: "this is because small fish (e.g. anchovy, sardine, herring) appear to keep jellyfish in check by predation (on young jellyfish when they are very small) and competition (for the same zooplankton food). So, once we remove fish, jellyfish can proliferate."

As an example Richardson points to Namibia where "intense fishing has decimated sardine stocks and jellyfish have replaced them as the dominant species."

Eutrophication is another human impact in the ocean that is likely contributing to exploding numbers of some species of jellyfish. An increase in nitrogen and phosphorous in the ocean, eutrophication is largely caused by fertilizer and waste runoff seeping into the oceans. This leads to algae blooms, which lower oxygen in the marine ecosystem, creating so-called "dead zones". Dead zones have been increasing dramatically around the world, giving jellyfish another advantage.

"Fish avoid low oxygen water but jellyfish, having lower oxygen demands, not only survive but can thrive in these conditions as there is less predation and competition from fish," explains Richardson.

Furthermore, Richardson and his colleagues speculate that climate change may expand the traditional ranges of jellyfish at the expense of other marine species. "As water warms, tropical species are moving towards the Poles. This has been documented on land and in the sea. Many venomous jellyfish species are tropical (e.g. box jellyfish and irukandji) and... could move south into more densely populated subtropical and temperate regions," Richardson says.

As an example the paper points to box jellyfish and the incredibly small irukandji in Australia. These fatal species often cause beach closures in their native northeast Australia, and there is a concern that as the water warms they will make their way to more populous southern Australia.

However, Richardson says that jellyfish explosions are species-specific.

"Only some jellyfish form large blooms and most do not—research is now focusing on identifying the species and their traits that cause large and problematic blooms."

Once jellyfish appear en masse in an ecosystem they make it very difficult for fish to stage a comeback. By feeding on fish eggs and larvae in addition to competing with fish population for zooplankton, the jellyfish successfully "suppress fish from returning to their normal population numbers," says Richardson, adding that, "one can thus think of two alternate states with each being stable: one dominated by fish and the other by jellyfish. Unfortunately, when there is a jellyfish dominated state then this does not support as much biomass of higher trophic levels of fish, marine mammals, and seabirds."

In other words, an ecosystem that loses fish also loses the species that depend on them for survival.

The study describes this state as a "monoculture of jellyfish," an apt analogy since the situation shares similarities with other monocultures. When a tropical forest is replaced by a monoculture plantation such as palm oil or rubber trees, an area of tremendous life becomes a desert in biodiversity terms, as do ocean ecosystems when jellyfish become the dominant species.

Jellyfish joyrides cause other problems, such as, bizarrely, disabling power plants. Some nuclear power plants depend on inhaling seawater for cooling, but in recent years a number of plants have got more than they bargained for. In 2011 alone, four power plants—one in the UK, one in Japan, and two in Israel—had to shut down after jellyfish swarms clogged the pipes that bring in seawater for cooling. This is not malice from the jellyfish, but simple physics: they are literally sucked into the pipes.

"We need to start managing the marine environment in a holistic and precautionary way to prevent more examples of what could be termed a 'jellyfish joyride'," Richardson says. Due to the difficulty of turning an ecosystem around once jellyfish have gained the upper hand, Richardson and his colleagues suggest focusing on "prevention rather than a cure."

They recommend a halt to overfishing small fish that are vital to keeping jellyfish in check such as sardines, anchovies, and herring; reducing the amount of fertilizer and sewage running off into the oceans, thereby mitigating dead zones; and finally confronting climate change.

"Cut our greenhouse gas emissions," Richardson says. "This would reduce the likelihood of venomous tropical species, such as box jellyfish and irukandji, moving into subtropical and temperate areas."

Certainly, all of these recommendations would aid marine biodiversity and ocean productivity in other ways beyond stemming the jellyfish take-over. But, if not tackled, a future ocean of jellyfish could have dire economic, social, and, of course, ecological repercussions.

While jellyfish are edible, it is doubtful that they could be as rich—or as diverse—a food source as marine fish. Richardson, who has tried jellyfish says "the best types are slightly crunchy.

Not a strong taste and usually had with a sauce. Excellent diet food, as it has virtually no calories!"

Far worse than a civilization forced to turn to a jellyfish diet is a degraded ocean with few fish, big or small, predator or prey; an ocean that no longer supports birds in great flocks or marine mammals at all. This would be an alien ocean, better suited for (bad) science-fiction than our actual future.

3

Why top predators matter

Better to be an elk, a coyote, or a grizzly than a wolf. Better to be a sambar, an elephant, or a macaque than a tiger. Better to be a whale, a jellyfish, or an octopus than a shark. Such wasn't always the case. Not long ago—relatively speaking—being a wolf, a tiger, or a shark meant sitting pretty at the apex of the pyramid, riding clear at the top of the food chain. Invulnerable to being preyed on, these animals were practically ensured—barring disease or infighting—a long life of preying on others. For millennia, even humans were mostly afraid of these 'top predators'. For much of our history, it was probably more likely for Homo sapiens to be killed by a tiger than to kill one (though the same could not be said of the far less dangerous wolf). Of course, all that changed during the past couple centuries: the ongoing rise of human populations, the destruction of habitat, the invention of guns, and the industrialization of society have left the world's top predators—barring ourselves—in an increasingly unenviable position.

Wolves, which were once dispersed widely across four continents, have dropped 99 percent from historic populations. Tigers have plunged from an estimated 100,000 individuals to at best 3,500 today. And in just a few decades some shark species have seen populations cut by over 90 percent.

Gunned down, poisoned, speared, 'finned', and decimated across their habitats, few animals have faced such vitriolic hatred from humans as the world's top predators. In areas where large expanses of wilderness are under protection, the one thing that is often missing is top predators.

As many of the world's apex predator populations face collapse and even extinction, new research is proving just how vital these carnivores are to the ecosystems they inhabit. Biologists have long known that predators control populations of prey animals, but new studies show they do much more: from reining in smaller predators to protecting riverbanks, mitigating erosion and providing nutrient hotspots, it increasingly appears that top predators are indispensable to a working ecosystem.

Not easy being king

Top predators sit at the apex of an ecosystem's food chain: wolves in Alaska, tigers in Siberia, lions in Kenya, white sharks in the Pacific, dingoes in Australia, and fossa in Madagascar are all examples of top predators. Some top predators have been introduced by humans, such as dingoes in Australia or fox in the Aleutian Islands, while lesser predators—known as mesopredators—have taken over only after humans have extirpated the ecosystem's "top dog," such as coyotes rising in the US after wolves vanished. Either way, the range and population of top predators have changed drastically as humans have taken over the world.

In the continental United States genetic evidence shows that there were 200,000 wolves (*Canis lupus*) when Europeans arrived; today there are less than 5,000. Despite millions of dollars and years of conservation effort, wolves are present in only 5 percent of their historic range in the US. They are just holding on in Eastern Europe, still widespread in parts of Asia, and extinct in Africa.

The world's largest cat—the tiger (*Panthera tigris*)—is endangered throughout its entire range. Despite being one of the most recognizable and beloved animals, tigers are on the edge of extinction. The species is classified as Endangered by the International Union for Conservation of Nature (IUCN) Red List, while two of the six surviving subspecies of tiger are considered Critically Endangered. Few animals have received anywhere near the amount of conservation attention and funds as tigers, yet every year the great cat moves further away from a comeback.

Even when top predators bring in millions in tourist revenue—as is the case of lions (*Panthera leo*) in Africa—they still face a barrage of trouble. Habitat loss, prey decline, poisoning, legal hunting, and illegal killing by gun or spear have crippled the African lion. Though they don't receive the same attention as tigers, lion populations have dropped from an estimated 450,000 to at worst only 20,000 today. Recent reports state that they could vanish altogether from some of their best habitat—

i.e. Kenya's grasslands—in twenty years if more is not done to protect them.

To think such species are somehow immune to extinction is erroneous: three tiger subspecies (the Javan, the Bali, and the Caspian), two wolf subspecies (both from Japan), one lion subspecies (the Barbary), and the thylacine (*Thylacinus cynocephalus*)—once apex carnivore in Australia—all vanished during the 20th Century.

Other top predators linger on the edge of extinction: the Amur leopard, the Indo-Chinese tiger, the Arabian leopard, the Javan leopard, and the Asiatic cheetah could all vanish during this century. In some parts of the world, populations of large mammalian carnivores have dropped a staggering 95-99 percent.

It's not just on land where top predators are vanishing. In the oceans, sharks, once indomitable, are facing perils probably comparable to any extinction event over their last 400 million years on the planet. Overfishing, by-catch, and 'finning' (whereby fishermen cut off a shark's fin and then dump the animal back in the water, where it soon succumbs) are all taking a toll on a number of sharks. A study in 2006 found that up to 73 million sharks are killed by finning in a single year—all this to keep up orders of the Asian delicacy: shark fin soup. The first global survey of sharks and rays found that nearly one in three species is threatened with extinction, a percentage nearly comparable to amphibians, which are said to be in the midst of an extinction crisis. Already, in the last sixty years, the world has lost the Caribbean monk seal (*Monachus tropicalis*) to human hunting and more recently, the baiji (*Lipotes vexillifer*), a top predator and river dolphin of China's Yangtze River.

While top predators are vanishing worldwide, recent research papers show a very new, and surprising, side to these megafauna. Peeling off the dangerous, fierce veneer, these studies find that top predators are actually protectors of the ecosystems they inhabit.

'My enemy's enemy is my friend'

It has long been known that top predators impact, and in many ways manage, populations of prey species (such as wolves and elk, lion and zebra, tigers and deer), but recent studies have shown that top predators also greatly affect carnivorous species one rung beneath them in the food chain, known as mesopredators. Coyotes in North America, hyenas in Africa, ocelots and jaguarundis in South America, and weasels in Europe are just a few examples of the global menagerie of mesopredators.

A 2009 paper in Ecology Letters titled "Predator interactions, mesopredator release and biodiversity conservation" reviewed 94 top predator-mesopredator studies, discovering just how great an impact top predators have on those beneath them, and in turn many other species on down the food chain.

Mesopredators are often "versatile generalist hunters, with a capacity to reach high population densities and have large impacts on a wide range of prey species" according to the paper. 'Meso' in Ancient Greek means simply middle or intermediate.

Euan Ritchie, lead author of the paper, outlined two ways in which top predators impact lesser mesopredators, dubbing them "fear and loathing."

"First of all," he says, "top predators loathe mesopredators (think dogs and cats), perhaps through perceived competition and therefore they often actively seek them out and kill them, thereby reducing the overall abundance of mesopredators."

According to the paper this "loathing" sometimes leads a top predator to kill a smaller one "for food and to eliminate an ecological competitor." Some top predators will even kill a mesopredator and leave the body without consuming it: loathing, to an extreme.

It should not be surprising, then, that there are few things in the world mesopredators fear more than a run-in with a top predator: studies have shown that fear alone causes significant behavioral shifts in mesopredators.

"Fear may cause mesopredators to reduce or change their times of activity and/or habitats they use," Ritchie, with Deakin University in Melbourne, explains. "This can lead to the reduced ability of mesopredators to find food, therefore lowering reproduction and survival, and hence can have large impacts on their populations."

The inverse is also true: a reduction in top predators allows mesopredators to increase disproportionately, sometimes as much as fourfold, according to the review. In other words if a wolf population drops by a hundred that may allow, under certain conditions, the coyote population to explode by as much as four hundred. This ecological occurrence, termed 'mesopredator release' by scientists, does not occur unnoticed in the ecosystem, but has profound impacts all down the food chain.

As Ritchie explains: "When top predators are removed from an environment (e.g. dingoes), mesopredators (e.g. cats or foxes), which tend to be more generalist and opportunistic species with a high reproductive rate relative to larger predators, can quickly increase in abundance and drive prey species to extinction," adding that, "this is especially true where the prey species themselves have quite low reproductive rates, such as many of Australia's native mammals."

As an example, a population of rufous hare-wallaby (*Lagorchestes hirsutus*) vanished in Australia following the poisoning of local dingoes. Once the dingoes were gone, foxes (an alien species in Australia) invaded the area and the rufous hare-wallabies, who had survived side-by-side with the dingo for centuries, were quickly hunted out of existence. Currently, the rufous hare-wallaby is listed as Vulnerable by the IUCN Red List.

In cases such as this, top predators actually ensure the survival of certain prey species. By keeping a constant check on mesopredators, top predators in turn become protectors of prey species, especially smaller prey. It may not be too much of a stretch to label the world's top predators: 'guardians of the small'.

"In short," Ritchie says, "my enemy's enemy is my friend."

And when prey overlaps between top predator and meso-pedator, Richie says the smaller prey would still rather keep the top predator at the helm.

"Even if large predators also occasionally eat the same prey species as mesopredators, their impact is lower relative to mesopredators, due to their larger territories and smaller overall population sizes."

Although there is a general trend of top predators keeping a check on mesopredators—and thereby aiding a number of small species that would be overrun if mesopredators are "released"—studying the relationship between top predators and mesopredators can prove incredibly complex. According to the paper, some underlying factors that need to be considered include resource availability, habitat types, and the relationship between various predator groups.

To illustrate this, Ritchie points again to Australia where the relationship among dingoes, foxes, and cats muddles the norm. Interestingly, all of these are invasive species, though dingoes have been in Australia for several thousand years. Dingoes are the top predator, and as such they kill foxes and cats. So far, so good. But foxes also kill cats—and there are more foxes than dingoes.

"The problem is that in some circumstances, by killing foxes, dingoes may be indirectly helping cats," Richie says—and few invasive mesopredators are more devastating to native fauna, especially birds, than feral cats.

"No study has yet been able to resolve the complexity of this relationship. There's no doubt the same situation could apply to other groups of predators, such as wolves, coyotes and cats/foxes/raccoons/skunks etc. We're only now beginning to delve into the true complexity of these relationships," he says.

Despite the complexity, Ritchie and colleagues have found considerable and varied evidence of the top predators' role in regulating the ecological system. Harmonious is one way to describe an ecosystem that still has its top predators. Not, of course, harmonious in the ideal sense of lacking violence—there is still blood and death—but harmonious in that the pieces work together like a symphony.

How predators protect plants

Top predators impact prey populations, the mesopredators below them, and—indirectly—the mesopredators' prey species, but how could the world's most efficient carnivores, whose very name comes from the Latin word carnivorum meaning 'to devour flesh', have any impact on plants?

At first glance it appears ridiculous that a top predator could drastically impact an ecosystem's plant diversity. However, a number of recent studies have shown just that: for example, a 2009 study in Biological Conservation of five National Parks in the U.S. (Olympic, Yosemite, Yellowstone, Zion, and Wind Cave) illustrates just how much plants, and thereby the health of ecosystems, rely on big predators. Not only could they be called "guardians of small prey species" but in addition "guardians of native flora." In fact, top predators' role as plant protectors may be their most important.

During America's short history, top predators—wolves and cougars—were largely wiped out from their habitats due to hunting, trapping, poisoning, and even government campaigns established to eradicate these 'pests'. But the study, along with a number of others, shows that the decline—and in many places complete expiration—of top predators decimated historic plant communities.

"The removal of top predators from landscapes allows, via reduced predation and predation risk, unimpeded foraging by large herbivores such as elk and deer," Robert Beschta, lead author of the paper, explains. "Heavy utilization of plants by these animals, over time, can greatly alter the composition of plant communities and thus impact other animals that are dependent upon these plants as part of their life cycles."

As an example, he says "in areas where wolves have been extirpated, greatly increased foraging pressure by elk on aspen, cottonwood, and willows can occur. If high levels of foraging continue year-after-year, this can eventually lead to the local extinction of these plants and others."

In other words, when the wolf is away (and in the cases of these parks he was away for at least half a century), the elk will play. But the elk's free rein—free both of violent death and fear—means no plants are off-limits from being consumed, and that means the rich plant communities that used to cover the park, including trees, face inevitable decline.

Excessive grazing by big herbivores "can fundamentally alter the capability of native plant communities to function in a normal manner," say Beschta with Oregon State University. He adds that, "unimpeded herbivory is a powerful ecological 'force' that can have profound consequences to terrestrial and aquatic ecosystems."

Scientists call this process a 'trophic cascade', which Beschta says "is used to denote effects of predators upon their prey and, in turn, upon plants."

Beschta, and co-author William J. Ripple, director of Oregon State University's Trophic Cascades Program, found in the five parks that twenty years after top predators were killed off, tree recruitment (i.e. the number of trees surviving to designated height) plunged to 10 percent of the amount required to maintain past tree communities. Within fifty years, the effect was even more acute: recruitment levels had dropped to 1 percent. Eventually, the authors write, this trend would lead to the local extinction of many native tree species.

After carefully eliminating other possible impacts, such as climate, fires, decline in impact by Native Americans, and land use, the study concludes that the plunge in tree survival was due directly to the decimation of top predators.

"None of the alternative factors explained the observed long-term declines in tree recruitment," the researchers write.

The loss of these plant communities affects everything in the ecosystem, from erosion to fire.

"Accelerated erosion of hill-slope soils or of stream banks can occur as the diversity and biomass of plant communities are increasingly affected," explains Beschta. In addition, "fire is an important mechanism for rejuvenating aspen stands but, in the presence of high levels of herbivory, fire accelerates the removal of large trees while sprouts and seedlings are unable to grow above the browse level of elk or deer."

In other words, fire kills large trees, which are unable to be replaced because herbivores quickly take out any youngster. Any gardener in the US knows just how destructive a single deer can be.

The loss of top predators—and the uptick of herbivore grazing—also has massive impacts on river environments, including undercutting riverside plant communities to a point where they "may be no longer capable of maintaining stable stream banks during periods of high flow," says Beschta. "Once riparian [riverside] plant communities are degraded, increased channel widening or channel down-cutting can occur."

Without trees helping to hold them in place, the banks simply vanish when the river rises. Such impacts can also increase sediment runoff, raise summer water temperatures due to shallower streams and lack of shade, and destroy important fish-rearing habitat.

A previous study in Zion National Park proves just how far the loss of top predators ripples outward: abundance measurements for a number of species—including water plants, wildflowers, amphibians, lizards, and butterflies—were lower in areas where mountain lions were scarce and more abundant in areas where mountain lions still roamed frequently. The presence of mountains lions boosted biodiversity.

Sharks, like their terrestrial brothers, have similar impacts. Where sharks are abundant, dugongs—large, aquatic, mammalian herbivores—are forced by the ecology of fear to move their grazing areas just like elk. This allows seagrass meadows to recover, providing habitat for a host of marine biodiversity, both plant and animal.

Top predators also shape freshwater ecosystems. In Oklahoma, researchers have found that large-mouth and spotted bass protect algae in streams by eating minnows that would otherwise decimate algae communities.

In the end, the loss of top predators can actually be linked to an overall decrease in ecosystem services.

"A diversity of native plant species, as well as the composition and structure of plant communities, are necessary to provide food-web support, maintain habitat, contribute to soil development, and a variety of other ecosystem services," explains Beschta. "The key to maintaining 'ecosystem services' is a healthy and vibrant plant community."

And the key to many biodiverse plant communities' survival, oddly enough, is the world's biggest meat-eaters.

Predators enrich the ecosystem

The deeper biologists delve into the book of life, the larger the role apex predators play, until these animals, rather than being the villain of the piece, become heroic, become kings again as they were to the earliest peoples. In fact, one of the most surprising recent studies on top predators—again with wolves as an example—shows that not only do they affect plant species, but also through hunting they actually create nutrient hotspots that allow for mini-explosions of life, keeping ecosystems rich and varied.

Using a 50-year-record of moose kills by wolves on Isle Royale National Park, an island in Lake Superior, researchers from the Michigan Technological University found that moose corpses create hotspots of forest fertility by enriching the soil with biochemicals.

Comparing the chemical composition of soils in kill sites to control sites, the scientists found that the soils of kill sites were 100 to 600 percent richer in inorganic nitrogen, phosphorous, and potassium than control sites. In addition, the wolf kill sites show an average of 38 percent more bacterial and fungal fatty acids; while nitrogen levels in foliage at kill sites were 25 to 47 percent higher than in control sites. This is the very stuff of life, providing an infusion of natural fertilizer.

"This study demonstrates an unforeseen link between the hunting behavior of a top predator—the wolf—and biochemical hot spots on the landscape," said Joseph Bump, an assistant professor in Michigan Tech's School of Forest Resources and Environmental Science and lead author of the paper. "It's important because it illuminates another contribution large predators make to the ecosystem they live in and illustrates what can be protected or lost when predators are preserved or exterminated."

Bump says he and his colleagues were shocked by just how clear the biochemistry of the kill was, especially considering wolves—with the help of scavengers—pick a corpse clean.

"We suspect that the stomach contents are important in creating the fertilization effects because wolves and scavengers do not eat the decomposing plant material and microbial soup in the stomachs of moose," Bump told mongabay.com.

If it is in fact the stomach contents that serve as the primary source of the rush of nutrients added to the ecosystem, Bump says that human hunters likely provide a similar uptick in nutrients. However, Bump adds that there is a major difference between wolf hunters and human ones.

"[Human-left] gut piles occur in different places and at different times of the year than wolf-killed prey. [Human] left gut piles are highly concentrated temporally during the hunting season, and are generally much closer to roads."

In other words, wolves play an important role in the distribution—both in space and time—of nutrient hotspots. According to the paper: "in contrast [to human hunters], wild predators hunt continuously and across a broader range."

"Wolf-killed moose were found in some areas of the study landscape at 12 times the rate of occurrence for moose that died from other causes," Bump says. "This means that wolves, in part, are shaping where a moose hits the ground. In some areas, in which wolves apparently have greater kill success, more moose carcasses are deposited and the soil changes we observed are highly clustered."

By clustering their kills, wolves create areas of great soil fertility that enhance the ecosystem—and this clustering isn't reproduced by human hunting, car collisions, starvation, or other means of moose mortality.

According to the paper, similar results very likely occur where other top predators hunt big prey.

"For example, we have observed similar above- and below-ground biogeochemical effects at elk carcass sites in Yellowstone National Park, U.S.A. [...] In the low resource environment of the Arctic tundra, the impact of a muskox (*Ovibos moschatus*) carcass on surrounding vegetation was still dramatic after 10 years, which emphasizes that carcass effects may last longer in some systems. Similar dynamics likely occur in South American, African, and Asian systems with intact large carnivore–ungulate prey relationships."

It would be interesting, certainly, to reproduce the study with lions in Africa, tigers in Asia, and jaguars in South America, among other top predators. It may be that through killing, top predators fertilize the soil around the world, bringing life from death.

The writers say this research is vital because it demonstrates an unknown and unexpected ecosystem service provided by top predators, which in scientific parlance is described as "creating ecosystem heterogeneity at multiple scales".

"What is important," concludes Bump, "is that wolves are not intuitively connected to dirt and how fertile a spot of dirt may be. Identifying and describing such connections tells a more complete story of what we have when we have healthy moose and wolf populations on the landscape. If ecologists continue to tell such stories then we will understand what is lost or gained with wolf expiration or restoration respectively."

Research in Yellowstone has also documented how wolf kills, in addition to providing a microbial soup that allows explosions of life, aid another group of organisms not yet mentioned: scavengers. The end of an elk's life in Yellowstone attracts all kinds of opportunists, from birds (ravens, eagles, magpies) to mammals (grizzlies, black bears, lynx, wolverine, and coyotes) among others.

However, when wolves were absent the biggest elk-killer in the landscape was harsh winters. This meant that scavengers did well only every few years: harsh winters provided a bonanza, while mild winters (now more common with climate change) meant hardship for scavengers, perhaps starvation or lower reproduction rates. But when the wolf returned—and replaced winter as the number one killer of elk—scavengers were able to have food no matter the seasonal conditions.

"I call it food for the masses," Ed Bangs, wolf recovery coordinator for the U.S. Fish and Wildlife Service, told YellowstonePark.com. "Beetles, wolverine, lynx and more. It turns out that the Indian legends of ravens following wolves are true; they do follow them because wolves mean food."

'Humankind's most pervasive influence on nature?'

In the hugely popular animated film The Lion King, lions, as the title suggests, rule the African savannah. But when the rightful king lion is murdered, a villainous lion takes over and brings with him a new age—one dominated by mesopredator hyenas, not lions. He kicks the prince—the true heir—out. We do not see the kingdom for a number of years, but when the viewer returns it is a wasteland. Vegetation is gone, the lush biodiversity is absent, and the remaining animals are starving. Timon, the wise-cracking meercat, says 'talk about your fixer-upper.' Of course, by the end of the film, the prince kills the usurper and the ecosystem returns to its former glory. It is fixed up.

Whether or not Disney writers had top predator ecology in their minds when they wrote the script, I don't know, but this certainly represents a wonderfully dramatized version of how ecosystems transform when top predators are lost. Of course, it's not meant to be accurate science, but as art it enlivens the sense of transformation when the rightful king (top predators) are overthrown and the subjects (in this case mesopredators) take over. Nature has more feudalism than democracy in it, and ecosystems fall into anarchy when kings are overthrown.

In fact, a 2011 review of recent top predator research, as well as other apex consumers (i.e. big herbivores), declared boldly: "the loss of these animals may be humankind's most pervasive influence on nature." While such a statement is certainly debatable, it does point to just how much humans have underestimated the importance of ecosystem kings.

For predators, the review looked at a wide-swath of top carnivores, including mountain lions, wolves, jaguar, harpy eagles, lions, leopards, dingoes, trout, bass, cod, sea otter, and sharks, among others.

"We propose that many of the ecological surprises that have confronted society over past centuries—pandemics, population collapses of species we value and eruptions of those we do not, major shifts in ecosystem states, and losses of diverse

51

ecosystem services—were caused or facilitated by altered top-down forcing regimes," the scientists write in the review. Top-down forcing simply means that the top predator—or in some cases the top herbivore—is cut out and replaced by a lesser one, resulting as we have seen in a cascade of impacts.

"We now have overwhelming evidence that large predators are hugely important in the function of nature, from the deepest oceans to the highest mountains, the tropics to the Arctic," Ripple, who co-authored this report as well, said.

Some predator declines have led to even more surprising outcomes. According to the authors, a decline of leopards (*Panthera pardus*) and lions (*Panthera leo*) in Saharan Africa led to a rise in olive baboon (*Papio anubis*) populations. Large baboon troops have since invaded human population centers. The problem is that baboons carry an intestinal parasite, which can be transferred to humans. The loss of leopards and lions has thus resulted in an attack on human health. This is not the only case.

Big predators may even impact the spread of malaria. Scientists believe the abundance of big fish in freshwater ecosystems could mitigate malaria by preying heavily on mosquitoes that spread it. Fewer fish may mean more incidences of malaria, say the authors.

"These predators and processes ultimately protect humans," Ripple says. "This isn't just about them, it's about us."

The final end product of the lack of top predators on vegetation is visible on the Scottish island of Rùm. Wolves have been gone from the island for hundreds of years. In that time, deer have picked the island's trees clean until none remain.

Of course, predators don't always bring about harmony. The introduction of invasive predators into an area long free of predators may also have negative impacts. The study notes that the invasion of Arctic fox (*Vulpes lagopus*) and rats into some Arctic islands has decimated seabird populations and in turn hurt vegetation. This is because seabirds bring important nutrients from the sea to the island's soils. No birds equals no soil nutrients. Despite such outliers, scientists have overwhelmingly found that historically present top predators create a more diverse and richer natural world.

The surprisingly extensive impacts of top predators have been overlooked for a number of reasons say researchers. These changes occur on a large stage—sometimes thousands of square kilometers and include a number of species interactions—whereas most studies look at small areas or single species. The changes take years or even decades to become noticeable, and many of these top animals were already in catastrophic declines before scientists began studying their ecological role. Most importantly, researchers are simply in the dark about such ecological relationships until they are disturbed. For example, no one would have guessed wolves would have such an impact on Yellowstone biodiversity until the wolves were killed off and then returned.

"These interactions are invisible unless there is some perturbation that reveals them," Estes says. "With these large animals, it's impossible to do the kinds of experiments that would be needed to show their effects, so the evidence has been acquired as a result of natural changes and long-term records."

Where do we go from here?

While researchers are discovering more ways in which top predators contribute to working environments, predators continue to disappear at startling rates. So, where do we go from here?

One relatively recent answer is to reintroduce top predators into environments where they have been lost. To date, top predators have been reintroduced into a few select areas, the most famous example being wolves in North America. But the process of reintroducing such species is new, and the scientists are hesitant to recommend it unreservedly without first knowing the full picture.

"We need to take a whole-of-ecosystem view, and not a single-species approach," says Ritchie, co-author of the paper on top predator impacts on mesopredators. "It is inevitable that whenever we tinker with a natural system, there will be some winners and some losers. So before we go ahead and change things, we need to ask why are we doing this, what do we hope to achieve, and what are the likely results going to be? If we can't answer these questions then we shouldn't proceed."

Yellowstone National Park has proven an especially intriguing example of the effects a reintroduced top predator can have on ecosystems, since the wolf, the region's top predator, was absent for nearly 90 years. The park has become an ecological laboratory where scientists are able to watch in real time the changes wrought by re-introduction of a long-absent predator. Suffice it to say, discoveries so far have surprised everyone by revealing just how far-ranging and important top predators are to their respective ecosystems.

Following the demise of wolves in Yellowstone, Beschta's study found that aspen declined rapidly due to intensified browsing by group elk herds. During this time, elk culling programs were initiated to control over-browsing in Yellowstone and other parks, but none could replicate the effect of a top predator on the elk populations.

In 1995 and 1996 a cautious reintroduction began in Yellowstone National Park: thirty-one wolves were returned to the wild. Despite being controversial, the measure was quickly a success.

"With reintroduction of wolves into Yellowstone, the large carnivore guild is again complete," explains Beschta. "Within a few years following reintroduction, we began to document a decrease in browsing pressure and an increase in height growth of young willows, aspen, and cottonwood in some areas. This result is extremely exciting as it appears that this is the first time in many decades that such plants have been able to grow above the browse level of elk and produce seed for subsequent generations of plants. Observations by others indicate that beaver counts are increasing and small predators and scavengers may be doing better. In contrast, elk and coyote numbers have been decreasing."

One example of wolf impact on mesopredators—coyotes—comes from a study that shows Yellowstone has seen a fourfold recovery of juvenile pronghorn antelope (*Antilocapra americana*), which had been targeted by coyotes. Scientists also believe the wolf may help the Canada lynx (*Lynx canadensis*), which is considered threatened in continental US (aside from Alaska). But what role could wolves play? The rise of coyotes across American landscapes likely put Canada lynx in competition with coyotes for their prey: snowshoe hares. Fewer coyotes may mean more snowshoe hares, resulting in a return of the wild cat where habitat is present.

The resurgence of wolves also brought a number of long-absent species back to Yellowstone. One of the most notable is the beaver (*Castor canadensis*). Before the reinstatement of wolves, there was only a single beaver colony in the entire park. In 2011, there were nine beaver colonies. Why the change? Beavers made a comeback because willows, needed for food, returned along the rivers.

"Overall, the reintroduction of wolves appears to have initiated a 'reshuffling' of Yellowstone's ecosystem, a reshuffling that is continuing," adds Beschta. "Over time, we hope Yellowstone will provide an improved understanding of the extent to which top predators such as wolves may have influenced other ecosystems across public lands in the American West."

To boost these findings research from Banff National Park comparing wolf areas with non-wolf areas, has come up with similar results. Willows, aspen, and beavers are thriving in wolf areas, but barely hanging on in non-wolf areas. The research has also found that the American redstart (*Setophaga ruticilla*), a warbler, has been extirpated from non-wolf areas because it depends on willows.

Despite some remaining questions, Ritchie sees top predator reintroduction as one means to reestablish healthy, working ecosystems.

"In many situations our environments have been so badly degraded through human impacts, there is often the case to be made that we have nothing to lose and everything to gain from bold experiments. As an example, in Australia the Tasmanian devil (*Sarcophilus harrisii*) is in decline in its native range of Tasmania as a result of devil facial tumor disease. This animal also used to be on the mainland of Australia until quite recently. From ecological theory and anecdotal evidence we know that this species may be able to control foxes and cats, and therefore help some of our other most threatened species. So why not introduce devils back to the mainland? They might be able to reverse some of the damage currently being done by foxes and cats, with the added benefit of establishing an insurance population of the devil on the mainland, free from disease."

There are of course political pressures on both sides—pro-predator and anti—that complicate the issues. Many people—much like mesopredators—still fear and loathe top predators. One only has to look at the recent debate over allowing wolf hunts in the US to see how emotional the issue can become. While the reintroduction of wolves in Yellowstone was an ecological success, politically it has proved far less smooth. In fact, the return of the wolf to the west may be short-lived, as American politicians have successfully stripped the wolf from the Endangered Species Act (ESA) in the first instance ever of politicians—not scientists—deciding when an animal is ready to forgo protection. The wolf now faces large-scale hunting, proving just how maligned top predators still are despite their importance. No one knows yet how this latest experiment in human-managed populations will impact the remaining wolves and, in turn, the greater ecosystem. Yet, for his part, Ritchie suggests that by culling top predators, especially pack-leaders, one may worsen rather than alleviate predator-human problems.

"Many large predators (e.g. wolves) have complex social structures and behaviors, and by killing individuals, especially the older, dominant ones, we can have large impacts on how a group of animals behave," explains Ritchie. "In the case of dingoes, there is some evidence that by killing dingoes, we are breaking down their social structure […] In some cases where dingoes are being killed, dingoes actually appear to be killing more livestock than when they were left alone. This is probably happening because few old dingoes are left, which in normal circumstances train young dogs how to hunt species such as kangaroos. So in effect what you're left with is a bunch of rowdy, uninformed teenagers who go for the easiest target, which are often things like calves."

Currently, Australia is mulling reintroducing dingoes to some areas in order to help over-preying on endangered native mammals. Recent research has also suggested that reintroducing wolves into the Scottish highlands (absent since the mid-1700s) could help native foliage return, which is currently over-browsed by deer. Many political difficulties stand in the way of such reintroduction schemes; in the end it's not the science, but the politics that dictates where we go from here.

As Beschta says, "the underlying conclusion of our research is that loss of large predators has been incredibly important. Where we go next is up to society based on this 'new' information."

Rewilding with our biggest meat-eaters is a bold argument, but one ecologists say we can no longer ignore. Imagine a world where humans learn to value—as well as live alongside—wolves and tigers, sharks and lions. Imagine rivers overflowing with spawning salmon and lions rebounding in Africa, imagine sharks swimming unmolested and tigers roaring back from extinction, imagine the jaguar returning to the southern US and the wolf howling across its historic range, imagine this and one can see there is more pull to ecosystem restoration than simply a more productive, more diverse environment.

4

The camera trap revolution: how a simple device is shaping research and conservation worldwide

I must confess to a recent addiction: camera trap photos. When the Smithsonian released 202,000 camera trap photos to the public online, I couldn't help but spend hours transfixed by the private world of animals. There was the golden snub-monkey (*Rhinopithecus roxellana*), with its unmistakably blue face staring straight at you, captured on a trail in the mountains of China. Or a southern tamandua (*Tamandua tetradactyla*), a tree anteater that resembles a living Muppet, poking its nose in the leaf litter as sunlight plays on its head in the Peruvian Amazon. Or the dim body of a spotted hyena (*Crocuta crocuta*) led by jewel-like eyes in the Tanzanian night. Or the less exotic red fox (*Vulpes vulpes*) which admittedly appears much more exotic when shot in China in the midst of a snowstorm. Even the giant panda (*Ailuropoda melanoleuca*), an animal I too often connect with cartoons and stuffed animals, looks wholly real and wild when captured by camera trap: no longer a symbol or even a pudgy bear at the zoo, but a true animal with its own inner, mysterious life.

Although the majority of camera trap photos are bleary, fuzzy or simply show parts of an animal rather than the whole, some camera trap photos are on a par with the best in wildlife photography, capturing one thing that is truly difficult for photographers: a palpable sense of intimacy.

But as mesmerizing as camera photos are, they serve a purpose beyond the aesthetic. It's safe to say that the humble camera trap has revolutionized wildlife research and conservation: this simple contraption—an automated digital camera that takes a flash photo whenever an animal triggers an infrared sensor—has allowed scientists to collect photographic evidence of rarely seen, often globally endangered species, with little expense and relative ease, at least compared to tromping through tropical forests and swamps looking for endangered-rhino scat.

Researchers have used camera traps to document wildlife presence, abundance, and population changes, illustrating never-before-seen behavior and in a few cases catching unknown species. Camera traps are also beginning to be used to raise conservation awareness worldwide. What better way to connect the public to little-seen animals than with wild photos?

It must be noted that camera trapping is not new. The first cameras to capture wildlife free from human presence were taken by photographic pioneer George Shiras in the 1890s. Shiras used trip wires and a flash bulb to catch his animals on film, photos which were eventually published in National Geographic. The first purely scientific use of camera traps was in the 1920s when Frank Chapman surveyed the big species on Barro Colorado Island in Panama using the trip-wire camera trap, dubbing it a "census of the living." However, technological difficulties, including battery power, size of equipment, and the trip mechanism, left camera trapping for intrepid enthusiasts and not mainstream researchers for decades. Not until the 1990s did a camera with an infrared trigger mechanism become available, and today with the advent of digital cameras, including video, the practice of studying wildlife through camera-trapping has exploded.

The use of camera traps has led to a huge number of discoveries in the wild kingdom, among them documenting an Amur leopard (*Panthera pardus orientalis*) in China for the first time in 62 years; proving that the world's rarest rhino, the Javan (Rhinoceros sondaicus), is breeding, with a photo of a pregnant female; rediscovering the hairy-nosed otter (Lutra sumatrana) in the Malaysian state of Sabah; recording the first wolverine (*Gulo gulo*) in California since 1922; taking the first video of a bay cat (*Pardofelis badia*); documenting the incredibly elusive short-eared dog (*Atelocynus microtis*) preying on a caecillian in the Amazon; proving the incredibly rare Siamese crocodile (*Crocodylus siamensis*) still inhabits Cambodia, and snapping the first ever photographs of a number of species in the wild, including Lowe's servaline genet (Genetta servalina lowei), the Saharan cheetah (Acinonyx jubatus hecki), the giant muntjac (Muntiacus vuquangensis), and the saola (Pseudoryx nghetinhensis).

The technology was even behind the discovery of a few new species. Both the Annamite striped rabbit (Nesolagus timminsi) of Southeast Asia and the grey-faced sengi (*Rhynchocyon udzungwensis*) of Tanzania, the world's largest sengi (otherwise known as elephants shrews), were first found via camera trap photos. Bizarrely enough, sengis seem uniquely attracted to this remote limelight: in northern Kenya a camera trap has also gathered the first evidence of what is likely another new species of sengi.

More discoveries are expected as researchers undertake new and larger initiatives, including a study of tropical mammals in seven nations by The Tropical Ecology Assessment and Monitoring Network (TEAM), a video initiative to document the elusive wildlife of Sumatra, and a recent research program that will take camera traps as far as Antarctica.

What's out there?

There is simply no tool better for finding out "what's out there" than the camera trap. Within a few months of setting up traps, researchers can start to have a good sense of what large and medium-sized fauna reside in the area while conservationists can convey accurately what's at stake.

On the island of Borneo, Brent Loken, Executive Director with conservation NGO Ethical Expeditions, has been working to collect data on the mammals of Wehea Forest in the Indonesia state of Kalimantan.

"Camera trapping provides a window into a world that was previously only accessible to researchers or individuals with intimate knowledge of that species or habitat," Loken says, adding that the Internet has drastically changed society's access to such photos.

"YouTube is providing a method of sharing this information with the world. Recent videos posted to YouTube of Amur leopards from the Russian Far East, snow leopards from Afghanistan or tigers from Sumatra have provided opportunities for individuals to learn about rare and endangered animals."

Ethical Expeditions had a simple goal for its camera trap initiative: "to document as many different mammal species as possible in Wehea Forest." Along with camera-trapping the group also surveyed on foot, netted bats, and caught small mammals. In total, they documented 50 mammal species to date—nearly a quarter of the mammals found in the U.S. in a forest smaller than Barbados.

Loken says that camera traps have been especially important in Wehea Forest for proving the existence of elusive mammals.

"Without camera traps, we would not have been able to document species such as the binturong, banded civet, yellow-throated marten, clouded leopard and sun bear to name a few. Camera trapping is also giving us insights into the density and abundance of the Sunda clouded leopard, one of the least known cat species in the world."

For the first time many researchers are also getting baseline population data on tropical mammals and birds where only estimates, and often just guesses, were possible before.

"New data analysis methods provide researchers the tools to estimate abundances and densities for elusive species, something that was extremely difficult to determine only a few years ago," Loken explains.

Once a baseline is established, subsequent camera trap programs can help decipher how populations are changing in the face of human pressures.

"As forests are lost at record pace, it is imperative to gain a better understanding of the ecological requirements of endangered animals such as the clouded leopard and how distribution and abundance may be affected by habitat disturbance," Loken says.

For Ethical Expeditions, camera trapping went beyond documenting animals: the group is also using the program as an opportunity to train indigenous rangers.

Loken explains: "We currently have a team of Wehea Dayak rangers who are independently monitoring camera traps in Wehea, downloading and analyzing data and writing reports. We have found that camera traps are a great way to engage local people and train them as parabiologists."

Out of the thousands of photos snapped, Loken has been most surprised by the number of orangutans photographed on the ground, since these great apes are naturally arboreal animals.

"A few were genuinely interested in the camera trap, with one large male coming right up to the camera and looking at it," he says.

Taking a series of some of the best photos from Wehea, Loken set it to music and posted it for supporters online. He notes, "To date, we have received more positive feedback on this video than any other video we have posted."

The cryptic species

Let's be honest, if you travel to the Amazon you're more likely to see a jaguar (*Panthera onca*) or a lowland tapir (*Tapirus terrestris*) than a giant armadillo (*Priodontes maximus*). In fact, you're probably more likely to see a jaguar attack a tapir than a glimpse of the world's biggest armadillo. One tour guide described the species to me as more mythical than real. So, how do you study something you may never see in person?

"Camera traps enable us to document and supply irrefutable evidence of the presence of secretive cryptic species in a way no other method can," Arnaud Desbiez said. "By placing a camera in front of the burrow where I know a giant armadillo is sleeping I can get the exact time it goes out to forage and the exact time it comes back. I also get very close observation of the animal, which I simply cannot get [without the camera trap]."

Desbiez, with the Royal Zoological Society of Scotland, is conducting a camera trap study of giant armadillos in Brazil's great wetlands, the Pantanal. It's the first camera trap study focusing specifically on this phantom animal.

"Due to its cryptic behavior and low population densities, the giant armadillo is one of the least studied species of the Dasypodidae family. The species is highly fossorial [i.e. spends time underground] as well as nocturnal and therefore rarely seen," he says, adding, "almost nothing is known about them and most of the available information is anecdotal."

Desbiez's study is hoping to change this. Not only have his camera traps documented giant armadillos, but Desbiez also hopes the photos will prove fruitful in understanding giant armadillo behavior.

"Cameras can be set to trigger pictures in a rapid sequence. It is almost like having a movie. This can enable us to observe all kinds of behaviors. One of the objectives of this study is to document reproductive behavior of giant armadillos and we are counting on the camera traps," Desbiez says, adding that "the best part of cameras is that they provide irrefutable evidence, which is easy to show and share with others."

Desbiez and his team are even able to identify individual giant armadillos by light markings surrounding the individual's armor. One thing that Desbiez has already discovered is that giant armadillo burrows play a bigger role in the ecosystem than anticipated.

"We really did not expect so many other species to be using the giant armadillo holes [...] ranging from collared peccaries to tiny mice," he says.

One day he hopes to photograph a baby giant armadillo.

On the other side of the world, researchers are employing camera traps to document another incredibly elusive species, the pygmy hippo (*Choeropsis liberiensis*). One might think that given how easy it is to spot their giant cousins wallowing in a river bed, it would be relatively simple to find a pygmy hippo. But in addition to being much smaller, pygmy hippos occupy the dwindling thick rainforests of West Africa, not the plains of Sub-Saharan Africa. In fact, they are so cryptic that researchers only took the first photo of a wild pygmy hippo in Liberia in 2008.

Ben Collen, one of the expedition members, described seeing the first photo in a blog: "I think we all spoke at once. [One of our expedition members] whooped with joy, and then we had a round of applause. We excitedly flicked through the pictures to discover the hippo had returned."

Colleen is a research fellow at the Zoological Society of London (ZSL) and has worked with pygmy hippos through the EDGE program, an initiative of ZSL.

"Camera traps allow us to implement broader and more standardized monitoring networks across a wide range of species in a cost effective manner; gain new insight into the status and trends of species; and specifically link to one of the principal aims of our EDGE program: to implement conservation for Evolutionarily Distinct and Globally Endangered species," Collen says.

While irrefutably proving that the pygmy hippo still survives in Liberia's Sapo National Park was a major goal of the camera trap program, Collen says the number one aim was to "implement a long term wildlife monitoring program in [the park]. The camera trap survey was designed to detect wide ranging and cryptic species, and to detect change in occupancy over time."

Camera traps give researchers around the clock access to places they could otherwise not get to and allow them to monitor species with very little disturbance to wildlife, Collen says.

Camera traps have not only been employed to track shy insectivores (giant armadillos) and herbivores (pygmy hippos), but also long-unstudied carnivores. Recently camera traps set up in Gabon took the first publically released video of the African golden cat, the least known feline on the continent. Unlike the other cats of Africa, the golden cat only inhabits rainforest, making it incredibly difficult to spot, let alone study.

"The African golden cat has dominated my thoughts and energy for over a year-and-a-half now," University of Kwazulu Natal graduate student Laila Bahaa-el-din recently said in an interview. "When carrying out a study like this one, you find yourself trying to think like your study animal. This helps put the camera traps in the right place."

Bahaa-el-din managed to capture amazing footage of African golden cat sitting directly in front of the camera and another of the same individual chasing a butterfly. On watching the videos for the first time Bahaa-el-din says, "I felt, at last, like I was getting to know this elusive cat."

Bahaa-el-din says her research is focused on understanding how the wild cat fares in logging areas.

"The video footage I recently captured was actually in a logging concession in central Gabon. It is recognized as having high standards of sustainable logging practices and has a zero tolerance for illegal hunting," she explains. "At the particular area I had my cameras set up, logging had taken place just two years previously, and active logging was going on just a few kilometers away."

The camera traps in the logging area also took photos of gorillas, elephants, aardvarks, leopards, and duikers, as well as a number of small mammals, says Bahaa-el-din.

"It indicated that logging alone should not mean the depletion of wildlife."

Bahaa-el-din will next be comparing the abundance and diversity of mammals in the logging concession to pristine forest as well as a poorly-managed logging area. The evidence from the camera traps will eventually be used to develop a conservation plan for the African golden cat, which is getting its first taste of global publicity thanks to the remote cameras.

"Previous methods used for applying capture-recapture statistics involved physically trapping the animals, releasing them, and recapturing them. Not only would this be highly invasive to a species such as the golden cat, but it just wouldn't be logistically possible due to the animal's timid nature and difficult forest environment," Bahaa-el-din says.

Camera traps for conservation

While many camera trap programs are established for the purpose of scientific research, conservation groups have also embraced the tool as a powerful way of reaching out to the public.

"Most species shown in our [camera trap videos] are hardly ever seen (alive) by human eye, our videos give the term 'biodiversity hotspot' a meaning which is understandable to everyone," Marten Slothouwer says, adding that "the videos put Leuser on the map as one of the most important conservation area's in the world."

Slothouwer is running Eyes on Leuser, a video camera trap project in the Leuser ecosystem in Sumatra, which is being undertaken not for research, but for conservation publicity.

"Until now, almost no videos existed of most of Leuser's cryptic wildlife," Slothouwer continues, "our videos can make people realize that it's worth it to save this forest, because it's home to an incredible variety of species and there is no better way to show this than by video."

To date the videos have proven successful in drawing an audience: an August 2011 compilation has been watched nearly 5,000 times on YouTube.com.

"It is nice when lots of people all over the world see that Leuser is an exceptional place," Slothouwer says, but adds that it's most important that Indonesians see them.

"Only when local leaders and politicians take responsibility can something change."

The decision to go with remote video cameras instead of the more commonly used photo cameras wasn't difficult for Slothouwer.

"Videos have a strong power of expression, cost of distribution is low and it's understandable to everyone. Videos leave a stronger and longer lasting impression then a written pamphlet, and people just love to see videos of animals that have never or rarely been filmed before," Slothouwer says, adding, like Brent Loken, that he was impressed by "the numbers of viewers WWF attracts with video trap clips of rhinos and tigers."

To date Slothouwer says he has been happily surprised at the number of species recorded. So far, he has captured footage of 27 species with just 10 camera video traps over a couple months. This includes incredible footage of a great argus pheasant (*Argusianus argus*) displaying for the camera; a bright-eyed banded civet (*Hemigalus derbyanus*) with tiger-like stripes sniffing the ground at night; a Malyan sambar (*Rusa unicolor equina*) flicking water and mud toward the viewer before settling in for a nice soak; an imposing Sumatran tiger (*Panthera tigris sumatrae*) sniffing the video camera; the strange hedgehog-related moon rat (*Echinosorex gymnura*) rifling though the leaf litter; and a white-winged duck (*Asarcornis scutulata*) swimming with her chicks.

"I think the marbled cat (*Pardofelis marmorata*) in full color daylight is the most special video we got, and also the masked palm civet (*Paguma larvata*) is nice. It looks completely different compared to masked palm civets I've seen from other photo trap projects," Slothouwer says.

As a filmmaker, Slothouwer prefers traditional wildlife documentaries to video camera traps, however this is the only way to catch many of these shy species on tape. In addition he says, "[videos from camera traps] really have something mysterious and exciting, you never know what will show up and what will happen."

Slothouwer hopes the videos will make a long-term contribution to the protection of the Leuser ecosystem.

"The videos we collect can be used for several purposes, e.g. as a tool to reach a large international audience, to support conservationists lobby activities, for local education programs and to help to raise funding for conservation campaigns," he says.

Sumatra can use all the conservation help it can get, as the island—Indonesia's largest—has one of the highest deforestation levels in the world. According to a detailed report released by WWF, Sumatra has lost half of its forest cover since 1985. Approximately half a million hectares (larger than Rhode Island) of forest have been cleared annually, mostly for industrial palm oil and wood-paper plantations.

Nothing's perfect

Of course camera traps are not perfect: like any tool they have their advantages and drawbacks.

Arnaud Desbiez, who is studying the giant armadillo, puts it this way: "Cameras are not limited in time…a proper camera, appropriately positioned (avoiding direct sunlight), can remain active in the field for over two months. Camera traps are discrete and do not scare animals so you can really get excellent pictures of animal behavior that would be difficult to observe. [But] camera traps are limited in space. They can only gather information in the tiny area where their sensors are positioned…Therefore animals can easily go undetected and you need a lot of cameras (which are expensive) to properly survey an area."

The initial cost of camera traps is an issue, especially in developing countries, where camera traps are needed the most. According to Bent Loken, who is surveying the Wehea forest, a single camera trap ranges from $150 to $600, and that's before one has to purchase other equipment such as extra batteries, battery chargers, and SD cards.

Camera traps also break. Tigers, elephants, and other big mammals have been known to attack camera traps, sometimes doing permanent damage. In addition, in areas where poachers are a problem, scientists often lose camera traps to people who understandably don't like their photo being taken. Depending on the environment, humidity, rain, and extreme cold can be other issues.

In addition camera traps are only useful in cataloguing certain species, i.e. big to medium-sized mammals and birds mostly (though small rodents are often caught too). Bats may be photographed but are difficult to identify, since they are usually in flight. Small reptiles, amphibians, and, of course, insects rarely show up well enough to identify.

There are many things a camera trap can't do; and in the end nothing beats sustained human observation of wildlife. There's no way a camera trap could have achieved what Jane Goodall or Diane Fossey did.

The future of camera traps: Antarctica and beyond?

This year, camera trapping hit a new milestone: it started snapping life on its seventh continent, Antarctica.

Ben Collen with ZSL explains: "My colleague Tom Hart and I are developing a number of projects looking at the impact of changing climate, expanding fisheries and other threats such as the impact of pollutants, on penguin populations."

Colleen says camera traps became a logical choice of tool after encountering a dearth in broad analysis of penguin populations.

"Therefore, we started to think about ways in which we could get around this and try to expand the currently quite limited monitoring network, and came up with camera traps as a possible solution," he says.

To get the broader view of penguin populations over time, Collen and Hart have set up camera traps overlooking penguin colonies. However, instead of taking a snapshot whenever a penguin walks by, the camera takes timelapse photos to document important events in a penguin's season, "including timing of first arrival, first breeding, departure and chick fledging, as well as population numbers," Collen explains, adding that, "consistent measurements of these types of data over time will hopefully tell us how penguins are adapting (or otherwise) to the different threats that they face; principally a changing climate."

Bringing camera traps into Antarctica—one of the most extreme environments on Earth—forced Collen and Hart to develop some creative solutions to several problems.

"Batteries don't function well and lose charge quickly at low temperatures, and we can have issues with equipment freezing. We're trialing some different battery types which work well at lower temperatures, and insulating the equipment. Our ideal way of overcoming this would be to link up a solar panel—this could freeze over in the dark winter when nothing much is going on, and wake the camera up in time for breeding season, which is when we want the data," Collen says, who adds that they're still looking for just the right set-up.

But it's not just the extreme cold that's posing a problem.

"The other main issue we face is getting cameras overlooking penguin colonies to withstand the strong katabatic winds that are common in Antarctica. We've tried to solve this by placing the cameras on tripods, tied to matting, with several hundred kilos of rocks on top to weigh them down," Collen says. "We're also prodigious consumers of electrical tape to keep things secure."

Even if they conquer the Antarctic, there are still many places camera traps haven't been utilized.

So, why not aim high? A canopy camera trap could possibly document birds, reptiles, and monkeys in the rainforest canopy. Or low? Underwater cameras could document marine wildlife, in addition to the fauna of lakes and rivers. Perhaps with further technological advances, it may even be possible to use macro cameras to document the world's micro-species. The future of camera trapping may only be limited by our imagination.

Camera traps are just one of the many new tools—including GPS, satellite monitoring of deforestation, genetic studies—used by researchers and conservationists in a rushed bid to catalogue life on Earth in an age of widespread environmental degradation. However, those setting up the traps hope the tool will do more than just leave photos of animals behind. They hope the camera trap will be one new armament in the battle to save the world's species.

5

Nature's greatest spectacle faces extinction

If we could turn back the clock 200 years, we could watch as millions of whales took to their migration routes. Around 150 years ago, we could witness bison filling the vast America prairie or a billion passenger pigeons blotting out the sky for days. Only a few decades back and over a million saiga antelope could be seen crossing the plains of Central Asia.

Fast-forward to today: the humpback whale (*Megaptera novaeangliae*) population is only 5 percent of its estimated historic population. Based on DNA data, the species has fallen from 1.5 million behemoths to 80,000. Around 30,000 American bison (*Bison bison*) are left out of a population that may have reached 100 million; the percentage remaining is not even a whole number. The saiga antelope (*Saiga tatarica*) has dropped 95 percent in twenty years, from a million individuals to 50,000. But the passenger pigeon (*Ectopistes migratorius*) proves the most drastic, going from one of the world's most populous birds to extinct in a few decades. Such examples illustrate a common occurrence: the phenomenon of mass-migration going the way of the passenger pigeon. From whales to sea turtles and insects to songbirds, from hoofed mammals to the predators that track them, massive migrations are declining worldwide, and in a number of cases simply vanishing altogether.

In a paper in PLoS Biology, David S. Wilcove and Marin Wikelski, both with the Department of Ecology and Evolutionary Biology at Princeton, discuss the ramifications of such losses in abundance, and the importance of putting new conservation attention on beleaguered migrants.

Wilcove and Wikelski point to four major reasons why massive migrations are gravely threatened: human-created barriers like dams, fences, and roads; habitat destruction; climate change; and overexploitation of a species, particularly important in the case of oceanic and freshwater migrants. All of these reasons are anthropogenic (human-related), but Wilcove and Wikelski believe that those who caused the demise of the great migrations could also save them, arguing that the world's great migrations deserve suitably large-scale conservation initiatives. In fact, they state that mass-migrations should be protected much like endangered species. But unlike endangered species, massive populations of the migrating species must be preserved to warrant success, while researchers often consider a few hundred healthy breeding pairs enough for the recovery of an endangered animal.

Although no one knows exactly how each migration affects its environment, the authors believe diminishing migrations drastically alter the productivity of an ecosystem, challenging its ability to provide essential services. For example, the authors illustrate that salmon "by migrating upstream, spawning, and dying, transfer nutrients from the ocean to the rivers. A portion of the nutrients is delivered in the form of feces, sperm, and eggs from the living fish; much more comes from the decaying carcasses of the adults. Phosphorus and nitrogen from salmon carcasses enhance the growth of phytoplankton and zooplankton in the rivers, which provide food for smaller fish, including young salmon." However, the northwestern rivers of America receive only about 6-7 percent of the nutrients they once did due to a drastic decline in the migratory population of salmon. Fewer nutrients ultimately lead to fewer salmon in the next generation and less biomass altogether.

It is not just one-species migrations, such as salmon and saiga, that suffer from decline.

"Birdwatchers in North America and Europe, for example, complain that fewer songbirds are returning each spring from their winter quarters in Latin America and Africa, respectively," the authors write, citing a recent study of Europe's birds, which show migratory birds have suffered greater declines in population than stationary species. Such drops in population are also bound to have drastic impact on ecosystems; for example, migratory birds help control insect populations. Fewer birds may mean a population explosion of insects, some of which could be detrimental to forests or nearby rural land.

A 2005 study of the passenger pigeon's extinction argued that the bird's demise caused the current prevalence of Lyme disease. Deer ticks (*Ixodes scapularis*) only spread Lyme disease after feeding on an infected host, often mice. But mice, researchers theorized, are more abundant now since the extinction of the passenger pigeons. Why? Passenger pigeons used to compete with mice for the same food-source, acorns. Thereby, the loss of passenger pigeons may have caused an incomprehensible rise in the deer tick population due to more mice.

Of course, when migratory species diminish, predator numbers also decline as their food sources dry up. In addition, plant diversity and populations change when thousands of herbivorous mammals fail to make their seasonal appearances.

Illustrating just how imperiled global migrations are, a 2009 study in Endangered Species Research surveyed two dozen large ungulate species (hoofed animals) known for their migratory patterns, including some well-known species, such as caribou (*Rangifer tarandus*), American bison, elk (*Cervus canadensis*), zebra, blue wildebeest (*Connochaetes taurinus*), Tibetan antelope (*Pantholops hodgsonii*), and saiga.

Shockingly, all 24 focal species lost migration routes and suffered population declines. Six of the focal species either no longer migrated at all, or, in a couple cases, no longer survived in the wild: the springbok (*Antidorcas marsupialis*) used to form some of the world's largest migrations; the black wildebeest (*Connochaetes gnou*) was nearly exterminated and has relied on reintroduction efforts; the blesbok (*Damaliscus dorcas*) is not endangered but no longer migrates; the dwindling population of wild ass or kulan (*Equus hemionus*) of central Asia has been cut in half in just 16 years; the scimitar horned oryx (*Oryx dammah*) is extinct in the wild, but there are plans for reintroduction; and the quagga (*Equus quagga*) from southern Africa is simply gone for good.

Part of the problem has simply been a lack of awareness: researchers found that many of these migrations have been little studied. Although Africa includes the most large-scale migrations, the authors discovered that three migrating species had no publications on their population status at all. In Eurasia half of the migratory species have been largely ignored by science.

Preserving migrations, however, has proven even more difficult than identifying the causes in their decline.

"If we are going to conserve migrations and species, we need to identify what needs to be done: where migrations remain, how far animals move, their habitat needs and location, threats, and the knowledge gaps that needed to be filled," says co-author Joel Berger with the Wildlife Conservation Society and the University of Montana. "For some of these species, such as the wildebeest and eland in Botswana, threats were identified decades ago. We as a society have made little progress at figuring out how to save migrations."

Harris adds that "a large part of this is an awareness issue. People don't realize what we have and are losing."

But preserving thousands to millions of individuals will be far from easy. Wilcove and Wikelski write that saving these migrations will pose "unique scientific and social challenges". How does one approach preserving abundance, rather than settling for simple existence? The writers believe that protecting migrations will require action on the local, national, and global level. Those in power will have to change their mindset and protect a species before its population declines.

However, to date the importance of migrations has not penetrated the policy sphere. Even the world's most well known migration—the wildebeest in the Serengeti—is facing an existential threat from a road that could potentially cut off the movement of wildebeest, essentially stalling one of the greatest natural spectacles on earth. Warnings from the tourism sector, environmental groups, and international governments have to date failed to stop the Tanzanian government from proceeding on the road.

"If we are successful," Wilcove and Wikelski write, "it will be because governments and individuals have learned to act proactively and cooperatively to address environmental problems, and because we have created an international network of protected areas that is capable of sustaining much of the planet's natural diversity."

The authors believe it would be well worth the energy and sacrifices required, considering the ecological services provided by these massive movements, the scientific importance of studying the mechanisms behind such migrations, and the perfect wonder of such spectacles. Migrations are a kind of culmination of Nature's potential—once so prevalent across the world, now only surviving in a few aberrant places.

Some great migrations do remain. Although in decline, monarch butterflies still cross international boundaries in astounding numbers. At least for now, over half a million wildebeest, zebra, and Thomson's gazelle travel across the African plains, providing food for many of the Africa's large predators, from lions to hyenas to crocodiles. Caribou still migrate in the thousands across the Arctic tundra. And as recently as 2007 a previously unknown migration was observed in the Southern Sudan, with over a million antelopes, including the white-eared kob (*Kobus kob*), the tiang (*Damaliscus korrigum*), and the mongalla gazelle (*Eudorcas albonotata*).

Conservationist and adventurer, Michael Fay, said of the discovery: "This could represent the biggest migration of large mammals on Earth. I have never seen wildlife in such numbers, not even when flying over the mass migrations of the Serengeti."

Although on the wane, great migrations still exist: the discovery of a new migration, containing a million individuals, buoys that point. Now, with proactive attention, great energy and global cooperation, such migrations could not only survive, but thrive. In the future—as in the past—millions of whales, saiga antelopes, and even bison could move along migratory routes, completing their ecological role.

6

The penguin problem, or stop eating our fish!

Everyone loves penguins. With their characteristic black-and-white 'tuxedo' markings, upright waddle, and childlike stature, penguins seem at once exotic and familiar: exotic because they live near the bottom of the world, familiar because they seem to pop up everywhere. From Mr. Popper's Penguins to Happy Feet, from March of the Penguins to And Tango Makes Three, penguins star in innumerable books and movies. We grow up with them as children, along other animal media-star species like dolphins and lions. There was Feathers McGraw, Pingu, Tennessee Tuxedo, and Chilly Willy, who erroneously lived in an igloo in Fairbanks, Alaska. A tuxedoed penguin mascot, 'Willie' was even used to sell Kool cigarettes. In 2009, Entertainment

Weekly, a US periodical, honored the penguin by naming it in its decadal 'best of list' for the numbers of books and films the waddling flightless bird had inspired during the last ten years. Yet despite penguins' popularity in the human kingdom, few people seem aware that penguins—real penguins—are facing an extinction crisis.

Penguins receive far less serious media coverage than other 'favorite' endangered species—such as tigers, elephants, rhinos, and whales—even though the plight of penguins is as perilous as any of these. According to the IUCN Red List, over 60 percent of the world's 18 penguin species are threatened with extinction. If the 'Near Threatened' category is added, the percentage jumps to over seventy, and the ones not considered endangered yet may soon become so.

What is causing so many penguin populations to hit dangerously low levels? According to penguin expert Dr. David G. Ainley, the birds are plummeting because of competition with humans. Not competition over habitat, like most species around the world, but over food. Put simply: the industrialized world is eating penguins to extinction.

"The main threat is depletion of fish by industrial fishing," Ainley explained, "and all penguin species except for the Antarctic ones, whose habitat so far is protected a bit by sea ice, have been seriously affected by this […] Penguins need lots of food, nearby, reliably available. It's easy for fishing to negatively alter this."

A marine biologist who has been studying penguins and other top marine predators for decades, Ainley has especially focused on the Adélie penguin (*Pygoscelis adeliae*). The Adélie is one of a minority of penguins that is not currently considered threatened. Ainley says this is because the Adélie penguin is native to Antarctica and outlying islands. Despite the perception that penguins are an Antarctic animal, only four of the world's 18 penguin species breed in Antarctica, and only one—the Emperor penguin (*Aptenodytes forsteri*)—does so in the winter. The fact that Antarctic breeders are doing okay may be one reason why society appears to have little sense of penguins' problems.

"The Antarctic penguins are still very abundant and an appreciable number of reporters find their way to their areas. So, we get story after story after story about the penguins on the Antarctic Peninsula, to which lots of nature tours go, and little from elsewhere. Most of the other penguin species occur on offshore islands which are often harder to get to for the usual media story," Ainley explains.

After industrial fishing, other threats include human destruction of breeding areas, climate change, and pollution like oil spills. However, Ainley says that for penguins climate change is currently less disruptive than overfishing.

"Climate change cannot hold a candle to the changes that industrial fishing has already wrought on the marine environment. That's the inconvenient truth that even the climate change champions can't admit."

Ainley adds that climate change in combination with industrialized fishing will add greater pressure on the birds' food sources.

"Changed wind patterns, affected upwelling, altered ocean temperature, and eventually greater acidification [...] will affect the process way down in the food webs relative to where penguins occur in them," he says.

This has been borne out by a 2011 study in the Proceedings of the National Academy of Sciences (PNAS) which found that a staggering decline in krill was hurting Adélie and chinstrap penguins (*Pygoscelis antarcticus*). Since 1970 krill populations have fallen by 80 percent in the Southern Ocean surrounding Antarctica. Because krill require sea ice to reproduce, shrinking sea ice due to climate change has made it more difficult for the krill to breed.

"As warming continues, the loss of krill will have a profound effect throughout the Antarctic ecosystem," says Dr. Wayne Trivelpiece, lead author of the paper. "For penguins and other species, krill is the linchpin in the food web."

Just as with industrial fishing scooping up penguins' fish, here a warmer world comes to the same equation: less food, fewer penguins. Ainley says this is in line with penguin physiology.

"[Penguins'] very high energy needs make them very sensitive to food availability and other ecosystem processes that affect food. It 'costs' a lot of energy to swim in the ocean, especially the cold ocean where penguins occur. Since they don't fly, they are very poor at searching for food. Thus, it is very necessary for there to be a lot of food in known locations."

Penguins' role as predators, their need for an abundant number of food sources to survive, and the ease with which researchers are able to study these birds, make them good 'indicator species' of how the southern oceans—and especially the marine food chain—are holding up. Unfortunately the indications are not good: Ainley says that the industrialized fishing has 'simplified' marine food webs to the detriment of penguins and many other marine animals.

A number of penguins are also threatened by the increasingly desperate race for fossil fuels. Living on the southern coast of Africa, the African penguin (*Spheniscus demersus*) swims and feeds in one of the busiest oil shipping regions of the world. Two spills in the last two decades—1994 and 2000—killed a total of 30,000 penguins. However, the 2000 spill also resulted in the largest bird rescue ever, with tens of thousands of volunteers helping oiled and threatened birds survive. Like its relatives, the African penguin has also suffered from overfishing.

"Add to [the oil spills] the huge alteration of the Benguela Current, owing to fish depletion, and it is little wonder that this species is critically endangered," says Ainley.

Rockhopper penguins (*Eudyptes moseleyi*) have also been hit hard by a recent oil spill after a cargo vessel wrecked on Nightingale Island, a part of the UK's incredibly remote Tristan da Cunha archipelago. The spill coated 4,000 northern rockhopper penguins, but rallied the tiny community of 260 people to do everything in their power to save the birds.

Ainley warns that even more species of penguins could become threatened by oil spills as society's drive for ever more new fossil fuel sources leads industry further afield.

"If drilling ever happens on Falklands Shelf—and this must be the reason that Argentina and UK went to war, i.e. for potential oil—then a number of penguin populations there would be vulnerable," he says.

Five species of penguin breed on the Falklands, more even than in Antarctica. An oil spill near these islands could be catastrophic for the world's penguins. For now, though, the biggest threat to penguins globally remains industrial fishing.

Ainley says that people can help save the world's penguins by "asking for the establishment of marine protected areas, which are the only way to control the fishing industry and prevent the ultimate complete depletion of Earth's marine resources."

In addition he asks penguin-lovers to avoid purchasing Chilean sea bass. The rapid decline of Chilean sea bass has affected everything from whales to seals to penguins. There have even been reports of fishermen dynamiting killer whales and sperm whales to kill their competition for the species.

"As the penguins said in Happy Feet, which I thought to be a very good film, much more sophisticated and true than March of the Penguins: 'STOP EATING OUR FISH!!!'" Ainley echoes.

Perhaps the penguin's popularity has proven a double-edged sword. Maybe their ubiquitous appearances in cartoons and children's books, films and advertisements have also given these wild animals the stigma of fancifulness. Has it become difficult for the public to realize that penguins are flesh-and-blood living organisms that are fighting for survival, not just media darlings?

Imaginary penguins are usually depicted as charming, fey, and irrepressible; they are almost always the heroes of their story. Yet, we have largely abandoned the real inspirations for our penguin tales. If we want penguins to remain more than happy doodles, it will require changes in our laws and behavior. Large-scale changes in how the fishing industry operates, and where it can operate, must come rapidly. Such changes would help our entire marine ecosystem, from loveable penguins all down the food chain. Saving the penguins may mean saving our southern seas altogether.

Penguin Species Threat Levels According to IUCN Red List 2011

Endangered:
Erect crested penguin (*Eudyptes sclateri*)
Galapagos penguin (*Spheniscus mendiculus*)
Northern rockhopper penguin (*Eudyptes moseleyi*)
Yellow-eyed penguin (*Megadyptes antipodes*)

Vulnerable:
African penguin (*Spheniscus demersus*)
Fiordland penguin (*Eudyptes pachyrynchus*)
Humboldt penguin (*Spheniscus humboldti*)
Macaroni penguin (*Eudyptes chrysolophus*)
Royal penguin (*Eudyptes schlegeli*)
Snares penguin (*Eudyptes robustus*)
Southern rockhopper penguin (*Eudyptes chrysocome*)

Near Threatened:
Gentoo penguin (*Pygoscelis papua*)
Magellanic penguin (*Spheniscus magellanicus*)

Least Concern:
Adélie penguin (*Pygoscelis adeliae*)
Chinstrap penguin (*Pygoscelis antarctica*)
Emperor penguin (*Aptenodytes forsteri*)
King penguin (*Aptenodytes patagonicus*)
Little penguin (*Eudyptula minor*)

7

What if Noah had left behind the ugly ones?

What would you give to prevent the extinction of the humpback whale? The giant panda? The Siberian tiger? Okay then, what about the red-cockaded woodpecker, the striped shiner, or the Galapagos rice rat? To date wildlife conservation decisions have largely been a popularity contest with the most popular animals raking in both attention and funds. But is this how conservation should proceed? Should we save only the beautiful and the beloved?

The science of ecology has shown, time and again, that species interact in a complex and intricate web, supporting an ecosystem by playing a variety of roles. When a species is lost, the impact ripples through an ecosystem affecting other species far and wide. Meanwhile, many of our religious and moral traditions regard all life as sacred and vital: God ordered Noah to take every species on his boat, not just the cute ones.

Still, big conservation organizations focus more and more on the popular species. In 2010 leaders from 13 nations met to create a plan of action to save the tiger (*Panthera tigris*), including pledges of $300 million. While this is hugely laudable, can anyone imagine nations shelling out hundreds of millions of dollars to save the Cuban greater funnel-eared bat (*Natalus primus*), a species more imperiled than the tiger?

The bias of neoteny

Berta Martin-Lopez with the Autonomous University of Madrid has spent a part of his career attempting to untangle why a big cat receives more attention than an oddly named bat. Looking at public values when it comes to wildlife conservation, Martin-Lopez recently reviewed 60 studies looking at how much people are willing to shell out to conserve a particular species, known as "willingness to pay," to find a pattern.

According to Martin-Lopez, whose research included 50 species from four continents—though only one reptile and one invertebrate—it's not the utility of a species, the level of endangerment, or evolutionary uniqueness that most pushes people to save it, but the size of its eyes—and that is not a misprint.

"The economic value for biodiversity conservation is mostly explained by the eye size of species, which is an indicator of neoteny. Humans tend to conserve those animals with apparently neotenic features, such as relatively large head and large eyes," Martin-Lopez explains.

Neoteny means the persistence of juvenile features in an adult animal; in this case it translates into what the public usually deems as "cute." Think: the big-eyed slow lorises, which have become victims of the illegal pet trade due to their perceived cuteness.

Economic gain and loss also played a major, though still secondary, role. Animals that provided economic gain or sport, such as anglers' favorite fish, generally scored higher than other species. However, one factor that could doom a species in the public eye was a perception that the species caused economic loss, for example, if it preyed on cattle. Causing economic loss proved far more important than a species' ability to provide economic gains through fishing, hunting, or tourism. In other words, while a wolf may bring in millions in tourism, its impact on livestock would quickly negate that.

Scientific reasoning, such as the species' role in an ecosystem or the threat of extinction, came in dead last.

Martin-Lopez says that people will support such conservation efforts when they are informed about the intensity of a species' threats as well as its importance to an ecosystem. However, this is by no means easy since, as Martin-Lopez points out, "the public has a low level of understanding of what biodiversity is and why it matters."

He adds that part of the problem lies in the public's disconnect from the natural world.

"More and more there is a widening gap between people and nature... humans are losing touch with nature. James R. Miller called this the 'extinction of experience'," he says.

Most conservation organizations, and conservation in general, have tacitly accepted this dark state of affairs, choosing to work with species based on what they refer to as 'charisma', which basically means selecting species that easily attract the public (when I say easily, I mean the animal is striking enough not to need context to make it interesting for most people). Whales are massive and awe-inspiring, tigers are beautiful and deadly, polar bears (*Ursus maritimus*) are elegant and seemingly cute, elephants are grand and intelligent, lions (*Panthera leo*) retain the myth of kingship, dolphins are clever and sleek, and chimpanzees are obviously so close to ourselves that their protection is in some ways self-protection.

While reasons vary, a few 'rules' can be deemed from a list of favorite conservation animals. First, as Martin-Lopez, points out, it is best for a species to be neotenic—or cute. This, of course, immediately excludes two whole 'kingdoms' of life—plants and fungi—from gaining much in the way of targeted conservation efforts. In fact, to have a wildlife organization's focus, it is best to be a mammal. Perhaps as mammals ourselves, it is only natural that we gravitate toward our relatives. Birds are the next best, especially 'charismatic' ones like the bald eagle (*Haliaeetus leucocephalus*) and California condor (*Gymnogyps californianus*), though all birds find champions in the world's passionate birders; but reptiles, amphibians, fish, plants, and—least of all—insects are rarely made the subject of species-focused conservation efforts.

Second, it helps to be big, in fact the bigger the better; animals significantly smaller than ourselves are rarely noticed—unless they are neotenic. Third, the species should be active and energetic; we don't care as much for animals that seem to do little, unless, of course, they are cute like koalas (*Phascolarctos cinereus*). Finally, symbolism or metaphors that surround an animal may aid its stature. In general, we prefer predators to prey, intelligence to instinct, and, of course, beauty to ugliness. The core reason for conservation groups focusing on such species is obvious: people will donate far more money to save a panda (*Ailuropoda melanoleuca*) than a Tumbala climbing-rat (*Tylomys tumbalensis*).

Cynicism could easily set in when one realizes we are saving animals based on looks. But most conservation organizations put their faith in a trickle-down theory; in other words saving the big charismatic mammals theoretically benefits every species in their ecosystems: by conserving elephants and lions you conserve all of the species of Africa's plains or by saving whales and dolphins you protect the seas. I will label this as trickle-down conservation, and much like Ronald Reagan's dubious economics it is only marginally effective.

Nature is endlessly diverse and there are many habitats that have been wholly neglected due to the lack of any charismatic animal; for example, the Hispaniolan solenodon (*Solenodon paradoxus*), an amazing shrew-like creature that produces toxic saliva, lives in Haiti and the Dominican Republic, two nations that have received relatively little international conservation attention because of their lack of any high-profile animal. Whole ecosystems have been left behind all over the world. But that's not all: even massive conservation efforts in a nation don't necessarily mean every one of its species benefits. Kenya is one of the countries in which international organizations have sunk a lot of money to protect lions, elephants, and many other big mammalian species. Yet such protection has not stopped the unique antelope, hirola (*Beatragus hunteri*), from becoming one of the most endangered mammals in the world, simply because it inhabits a region apart from the African savannah.

Finally, conserving mammals and a few majestic birds does not mean other orders of life will be saved. Saving jaguars only translates into helping frog populations if frogs are suffering only from habitat loss. With any other threat—the illegal pet trade, disease, climate change—helping jaguars won't help the Amazon's frogs. Protecting whales does not stop shark-finning, the overfishing of tuna, or acidification of coral. Creating a park in Southeast Asia does not protect animals from the unsustainable bushmeat and traditional medicine trade, two trends that are creating 'empty forests' in the region, meaning that even protected, intact forests have been completely hunted out.

The truth is that imperiled species often require targeted actions. Much like trickle-down economics, trickle-down conservation mostly just helps the higher-class species.

None of this is meant to diminish the need to save such magnificent animals as the blue whale (*Balaenoptera musculus*) and the African bush elephant (*Loxodonta Africana*). Such beautiful charismatic animals still deserve the very best in conservation efforts, and without past dedication many of them would be gone. But the question remains: is popularity the measure of conservation? A new organization, EDGE, argues there is a better way.

A new response to cute first: the EDGE program

After a century of wildlife conservation, the ugly (and neglected) have a new champion. The Zoological Society of London (ZSL)'s new program, EDGE—which stands for

Evolutionary Distinct and Globally Endangered—works much like other small conservation organizations. It partners with local scientists, surveys populations, sets up conservation programs, and cooperates with governments and communities to ensure protection. However, what is unique about EDGE is not its approach to saving species, but rather the species it choose to focus its efforts on, such as the long-eared jerboa (*Euchoreutes naso*), Rondo dwarf galago (*Galago rondoensis*), saola (*Pseudoryx nghetinhensis*), sagalla caecilian (*Boulengerula niedeni*), atoyac minute salamander (*Thorius infernalis*), betic midwife toad (*Alytes dickhilleni*), elliptical star coral (*Dichocoenia stokesi*), and the parasimplastrea coral (*Parasimplastrea sheppardi*). Now, how many of those have you heard of? How many can you picture? Unless you are a biologist or a one-of-a-kind wildlife enthusiast, you may recognize few or none of these species—and that's the point.

By selecting relatively unheard-of species, EDGE looks to the future of conservation movements while reconnecting us to ecological, even to religious and moral, understanding regarding the immeasurable importance of all of our planet's inhabitants.

EDGE has come up with ground-breaking criteria to decide which species to focus on, based not on neoteny, but on science and need. Any animal—no matter how unpleasant or how lovely—will receive attention depending on how imperiled it is in combination with its evolutionary uniqueness. This means animal conservation should not be a charisma contest, but rather emphasis should be placed first on those animals that are unique, or in other words have no close relatives. The idea is that the more unique the species, the greater the loss if it goes extinct. With a possible mass extinction to rival the dinosaurs' on the horizon and only a finite amount of resources and time, emphasis must be placed somewhere. While such a criterion may sound as constrictive as beauty-is-best, it is not: the animals are selected objectively, through a mathematically determined score combining endangerment and evolutionary distinctness.

The result: to date 66 mammals and 85 amphibians with little or no conservation attention have been added to the small list of species that should not be allowed to enter the long dark of extinction without a fight. Starting by determining the top 100 EDGE species —evolutionary uniqueness combined with threat level—in a specific taxa (grouping such as mammals or birds), the organization than selects species that have been neglected. In the four years since its creation, EDGE has taken on grassroots conservation efforts with 15 neglected mammals, 33 amphibians, and 10 coral species through its special coral reef conservation program.

The organization has achieved several notable successes in its first four years: evidence that Attenborough's long-beaked echidna (*Zaglossus attenboroughi*) still exists in the foothills of Indonesia; the rediscovery of the Hispaniolan solenodon in Haiti; the first-ever footage of both the long-eared jerboa and the purple frog (*Nasikabatrachus sahyadrensis*); the rediscovery of the Horton Plain slow loris (*Loris tardigradus nycticeboides*) in Sri Lanka, including the first ever photos; finding a new population of Darwin's ghost frog (*Rhinoderma rufum*) in Chile; the first photo of a pygmy hippo (*Choeropsis liberiensis*) in Liberia; the good news that the bumblebee bat (*Craseonycteris thonglongyai*) is safer from extinction than initially believed; and the possibility of a new species of elephant shrew in Kenya. Given global press coverage of many of these discoveries, suddenly the world is seeing new animals on the brink—and who says a child can't be as fascinated by a bumblebee bat as by a panda bear (it's literally a bat the size of a bee!).

Looking back to move forward

With EDGE's incredible expansion of species worth saving—
including fruit bats, burrowing toads, and mushroom coral—
the organization is not necessarily achieving something new so
much as it is looking back. The idea that animals should not
be rated according to their usefulness, charisma, or beauty is
as old as the gods; in fact the reverence for nature may have
inspired the first religious cultures.

Even now, most philosophical and religious traditions press
for the equality of life. Buddhism teaches non-violence toward
every living thing, from man to the dung beetle. Hinduism, as
well, teaches an attitude of harmony toward the natural world,
not exploitation. In the philosophies and religions of Native
Americans, Aboriginals, Amazonians, and tribal Africans,
animals are portrayed as brethren to be treated with respect
and reverence with no talk in these cultures of eradication of
a species; all are seen as necessary to the whole. And all of the
Abrahamic religions (Christianity, Islam, and Judaism) contain
the story of Noah's Ark in which God orders Noah to save
every living creature from the flood. Never do Noah and God
have a discussion whether the weevil is worth more than a lion.
There are no 'deserves' in these multitudes of philosophies
and traditions; all life is sacred.

Unlike other issues where science and religion are seen as
clashing, science—especially the more recent discipline of
ecology—has begun to recognize such age-old truths. By
investigating the varied interactions between species, ecology
teaches empirically, as Buddhism does spiritually, that all
species matter.

EDGE reaches closer to this moral and scientific philosophy than previous institutions. Certainly, it must still decide to focus on particular species—it is bound by finite finances and support—but its system of selection is far closer to these moral traditions and scientific discoveries than beauty and cuteness contests.

The ambitious organization is working on expanding. Tackling birds next, it then plans to move on to reptiles, fish, and various plant groups. One hopes it will consider insects before too long; however, it depends on data from the IUCN Red List, which has long ignored insects as well as many other 'less charismatic' species. Once EDGE lists are developed, the selected species will receive the same attention as their mammalian and amphibian cousins. Imagine the impact of such a broad-reaching organization—so long as it receives the necessary public support and funding. And therein lies the problem: EDGE is testing whether or not the public will support a conservation group that doesn't just go for the easy-to-sell species. Time will tell.

None of this is meant to diminish the incredible work that other conservation organizations are doing and have done for the past 100 years—without them much would be irrevocably and pathetically lost. These courageous people have saved us that shame. But EDGE is just one new way of responding to threat of mass extinction.

It's possible that with new strategies, new awareness, new technologies, and most important, a major shift in values and philosophies, we can still sustain our planet's most unique attribute: life. Perhaps we are realizing it is not enough to save just the tigers, elephants, and whales; it is not enough to have a piecemeal environment. Such a place would be a decayed menagerie with humanity as apathetic masters.

No. Instead allow us to be bold. Allow us to be optimistic. Instead of saving just a part of our planet—bits here and there—allow us to press ahead and preserve the whole wondrous thing, from golden-rumped elephant shrews to long-eared jerboas, from bumblebee bats to long-beaked echidnas.

8

Zoos: why a revolution is necessary to justify them

A commentary

Watching a Siberian tiger kill a gray squirrel for a half-hour proved to be one of my most enlightening experiences at a zoo. It was a weekday in a Minnesota winter; I was alone, not even an employee passed by. The tiger pounced on the squirrel, flipped it into the air like a juggler's ball, pinned it, and rolled it. In a short reprieve from this unlikely encounter, the bloodied, half-crushed squirrel attempted an escape, dragging itself across the grass with a broken back; the tiger watched curiously, let it go a few feet, then pounced again. My whole self suffered over the squirrel's torture while marveling in the same instant at the tiger's power, the elegant feline ease with which it knocked the rodent along the ground. Here, in an institution where nature is faked, was a relatively truthful encounter: nature's brutality, grace, ugliness, awe, beauty, and tragedy were revealed. I never could conclude whether the Asian terror was just playing, or if it simply lacked the knowledge (as has been proven with some captive cats) to finish off the squirrel. Either way, it took a long time for the animal to die.

At 28 years of age I have spent countless hours in well over twenty zoos spanning four continents. I present this fact as the main expertise I posses in writing an essay analyzing contemporary zoos and their visitors. That is to say, this is not an empirical essay of a professional zoologist or biologist (or even a science major); rather this is one zoo-goer and environmental reporter's exploratory view of the current state of zoos and, more importantly and rarely discussed, some general ideas that could transform the zoo's place in our society. This is my hope. To avoid a discouraging length, I will not evaluate zoos separately (though of course they vary widely in quality), but rather sketch a general impression of the institution as it stands today.

The true purpose of zoos

Think about it: the zoological park in which living animals are subjected to strict confinement; where they must live a life that, no matter the size and 'naturalness' of the cage, is wholly different from the natural one to which they are suited; where their instincts are dulled, tamed, and corrupted (eating involves no hunting or foraging and sexual relations are interfered with and closely monitored) allows such seemingly needless suffering to fellow creatures that we, as (hopefully) ethical animals, must not only supply a very good reason for this subjugation, but also live up to it.

Zoos have a long history. China claims the first (as it does with most public institutions), but Egypt, Greece, and Rome all possessed zoos of a kind. However our contemporary zoos are direct descendants of Europe's first public zoos (replacing royal menageries built only for the aristocratic class). A product of the European Enlightenment, late 18th Century zoos were built to harbor animals for scientific purposes and public education. These were noble ideals, but it would be two hundred years before zoos began to consider the health and sanity of their inmates. At the same time, circa the 1960s and 1970s, zoos began to rethink their general purpose. It was quite clear at this point that the Earth was on the verge of a global mass extinction and only strong efforts by scientists and society at large could save the vast biodiversity of our planet. Contemporary zoological parks added stipulations regarding species general well-being, while embracing the idea that they must focus on conservation efforts worldwide and environmental education locally.

This is a purpose that makes sense. In fact, this is the only reason to allow such unnatural captivity: the zoo should be a local Conservation Center, focusing wholly on saving (or reinstating) species in the wild and on educating the public about the importance of conservation and biodiversity. AZA (the accrediting Association of Zoos and Aquariums) exists to make this happen, and there are many quality conservation programs within and coming out of most zoos. My skepticism lies not so much with zoo conservation programs (though I think there is always more that can be achieved on this end as well), but with their effectiveness as educators.

Zoo: the educational institution?

Zoos sometimes believe that captive animals themselves are sufficient education: somehow by seeing a bear in a cage one will be environmentally enlightened. Yet what do captive animals—lacking context—teach one about the natural world and its importance? The zoo is an artificial "wilderness": it is man-made and man-managed. There is no connection between a caged pen and an ecosystem. A visitor can look through the glass and see an insect, a snake, or a reptile and "learn" nothing more than this: they are boring, because they just sit there. In the same manner polar bears appear as playful, cute, and hardly menacing, though they can kill a two-hundred-pound seal (or human for that matter) with one blow from a paw. It's also not surprisingly difficult to wrap one's head around an animal being endangered when it's three feet in front of you. Without context—without quality information in a variety of forms—zoos only teach us illusions regarding nature and conservation, yet many zoos still believe that caged animals will say it all. If this were true, then according to my experience the main prey of Siberian tigers would be the North American gray squirrel.

Zoos have tried—a little—to incorporate education into the premier attraction. Some zoos are satisfied with including a fascinating fact about each subject: "the chameleon can look in two directions at once!" or "the kangaroo is the world's largest marsupial." Imagine going to see an exhibit on Van Gogh and finding that the placard below "Starry Night" only said, "He shot himself in the stomach!" Some zoos, however, have informative signs regarding the animal itself, including habitat, feeding, mating, nominal behavior etc. But even when zoos offer educational information, they expound on the subject as though the animal lives in a vacuum: zoos rarely explain an animal's place in its ecosystem. Better information on this level would allow people to find more respect for animals (or plants) they usually ignore and avoid—reptiles, snakes, amphibians, insects, arachnids, etc.—and to gain new insight into the so-called charismatic species.

A wide assortment of such information would help people understand why every part of an ecosystem is vital and why mass extinction is a deep concern, not just for those species on the edge of vanishing, but also for us.

Conservation and education

Since zoos embrace conservation as a goal, many include a display regarding a species' conservation status. Some are even enlightened enough to include the reasons behind the animal's endangerment. But when visitors read about logging in Sumatra or the bushmeat problem in Congo, what can they really do but shrug their shoulders in wonder and drop a quarter in a donation bin?

Zoos need to take these conservation issues and make them applicable. If they want to stop logging in Borneo to save the orangutans, why doesn't the zoo provide a list of tropical woods to avoid purchasing? In addition, why don't they highlight that the rainforest isn't being cut for Borneo's needs, but for western and Asian consumption? To tackle the bushmeat trade, zoos could address the larger issue of poverty in Africa. American policy can have a large effect on this issue. These are merely two examples of how to make wildlife conservation meaningful to the average visitor. The zoo, as a conservation center, must make visitors aware of their responsibility in fixing these global problems. For in the end it is lack of funds, awareness, resources, and will that continually allows our world to be ravaged in unsustainable and wasteful ways.

To truly reach visitors, zoos should employ a variety of new educational strategies: signs in front of a cage are simply not enough. To me it's always been odd that science and art museums have rotating exhibits, but zoos do not. Why not include such exhibits exploring a particular species, a famous wildlife expedition, or the state of our Earth? Imagine an exhibit on birds of paradise, the writings of Henry Thoreau, or the recent extinction of the Baiji. Quality and detailed exhibits may make some visitors excited by biology and conservation who are otherwise unimpressed by animals in cages.

Displaying exhibits on conservation issues would kill two birds with one stone (excuse the completely inappropriate adage). Such exhibits could cover major topics like human population, rainforest deforestation, or climate change. And if zoos are serious about shaping minds regarding conservation, they should be pursuing honest and effective information: the presentation should not wipe away the complexities of these issues nor avoid our responsibility in making the difference. Without including concrete steps the visitor can take to make a difference, the zoo threatens to worsen apathy, not aid awareness.

A theatre that played quality nature and conservation programs would be a perfect place for tired visitors to take a respite and learn something new. With amazing television programming such as Life and Planet Earth—including its follow-up episodes on conservation—and David Attenborough's wonderful wildlife series, it seems strange that zoos have not employed this as a novel method to provide both entertainment and education. However, if the programs have no focus on conservation and science, but merely display 'funny' or 'dangerous' animals to entertain, then they are not worthy of what should be a zoo's higher place in society.

While quality education may be lacking at most zoos, they are still doing great things in the conservation world. The Bronx Zoo, arguably one of the best in the world, is run by the Wildlife Conservation Society, which currently has 660 field projects around the world. The Association of Zoos and Aquariums (AZA) admirably brings zoos and conservation programs together around the country. But this leaves me with a question: why are these conservation initiatives not proclaimed? Why don't zoo visitors see information first-hand about what their local zoo (or zoos across the world) are working on? I'm not talking about just a little plaque and a few words, but an in-depth description of the project and its goals. Let the visitor know that zoos do not exist solely for visitors' needs, but as research institutes and bases for overseas and local conservation. Allow them to comprehend that animals are not mere entertainment for humans, but a vital part of ecosystems around the world that make our Earth as wondrous (and effective) as it is.

The green zoo?

Today, most zoos are standing contradictions. They use tremendous amounts of dirty power and water daily, both for guests and animals. Zoo cafes serve largely unhealthy and unethical foods. One minute you could be walking through a rainforest exhibit and the next drinking coffee or eating chocolate, both of which can be linked to rainforest destruction if not sourced sustainably. Or you might have just read about the devastating impact of climate change on amphibians worldwide and then have a hamburger or hotdog for lunch (while numbers vary, a 2006 UN report found that livestock are responsible for 18 percent of greenhouse gases released into the atmosphere). You can munch on some chips while watching orangutans and despairing of their plight without even realizing the threat to them and innumerable other Asian species is in your mouth—palm oil (which can appear in products ranging from snack foods to cosmetics and shampoo). The rise of palm oil has ravaged forests across Southeast Asia over the last few decades, especially in Indonesia (which lost 24 percent of its forest in just fifteen years) and Malaysia (6.6 percent). Or shop in the gift store and buy something—pretty much anything—and you'll be supporting China's industrial and booming economy run largely on coal, the highest carbon-emitting energy source in the world.

Imagine if a zoo put its ethics where its mouth is: power could be generated entirely from sustainable sources; water could be carefully consumed, reused after treatment, and collected whenever it rains; the zoo restaurant could be filled with local foods and carry chocolate and coffee that is both shade-grown and fair-trade (with explanations on the importance of these distinctions) and offering a selection of vegetarian meals as well as free-range meats, which have less environmental impact. In addition, the institution could make a point of carrying foods that either do not contain palm oil or carry eco-certified palm oil. The gift shop could sell materials that are only ethically and sustainably produced: instead of gifts from Chinese sweatshops or Indonesian rainforests, we could be buying alpaca scarves from co-operatives in Peru or hand-carved animals from recycled wood in Kenya. If a zoo cannot live by the standards it purports to teach, then our gluttonous society may already be beyond the point of help.

Obviously, many of these suggestions and ideas are dependent on funds. I am no economist but I imagine making a zoo 'green' would not be cheap. Nevertheless, I believe public benefactors and the government would quickly find funds for a 'green' zoo, and then tout that sustainability as an example to the public.

One zoo's incongruent decision

In 2000, the Minnesota Zoo—the state in which I grew up—decided to add a new attraction: a giant barn with lots of domesticated animals. Here is the description from the website: "The objective of the Wells Fargo Family Farm is to create a place for Minnesota Zoo visitors to become part of a community of people, plants and animals striving to maintain balance with nature." That's all well and good, but in what way does this meet the twin goals of wildlife conservation and education? These are not endangered species, but domestic breeds, genetically managed by and for man. These are not wild species: they have no habitat, no prey, no ecosystem—so why are they taking up a zoo's money and resources?

But this decision is worse for another reason. I have no qualms regarding the importance of petting zoos where kids can have direct contact with animals; obviously this is an important experience for many urban children. But Minnesota already has several places one can go for this exact experience: numerous small working farms that incorporate great educational programs for children and adult visitors. The decision by the zoo to spend $4.5 million on this farm complex is a direct threat to small family-farms that provide a similar experience in an authentic setting.

This giant barn also illustrates a final disturbing trend in zoos recently. You may have noticed the barn's evocative title: Wells Fargo Family Farm. Visiting some zoos now is like walking through a set of commercials: 3M, Cargill, Target, Walmart, Verizon, the list goes on. Even more ironic are the dubious, at times atrocious, environmental records of many of these corporations. Such branding de-legitimizes zoos, as though these animals could (or should) be "owned" by corporations.

I don't know how we reached a point where this must be said, but aren't we overwhelmed with enough advertisements without adding them to a public institution like a zoo? I do not look forward to the day when the library shelf sports an ad for Mountain Dew, the judge's bench proclaims Home Depot, and the church pew has Hallmark carved into its carpenter's wood.

Where could the Minnesota Zoo have better spent 4.5 million? How about updating old exhibits, additional educational facilities, creating a new exhibit on a particularly threatened ecosystem, overseas conservation, or how about a program that brings lower-income children and families to the zoo who can't afford the general admission price of $18?

A zoo is not a movie

Adults often view zoos as a place for children, as though we are too "old" to learn anything from encountering another species. Rarely thought of as a place for science or serious conservation, zoos are often seen by visitors, in general, as a form of entertainment, something akin to a fluff movie— and most zoos have bought into this. Yet for the sake of the future, zoos need to rise above their self-belief and the public perception that they are a carnival or a theme park, like Disney's Animal Kingdom, in which the line between theme park and zoo becomes so indistinguishable that animals are merely backdrops to the rides.

While our cultural fixation on entertainment and distraction is worrisome enough, it is a terrible thing when zoos place themselves in this category. To do so only perpetuates the idea that other species exist solely for our amusement and use (or abuse). Animals in zoos are not Disney characters; they do not speak English and tell funny jokes. Animals are true and real because they are not us; they are not slaves or property. I believe, personally, we have no claim (moral or otherwise) for mastery over them. Indeed, it was the expansion of this mostly-western philosophy of human dominance over pretty much everything that allowed previous generations to purposefully (or just lazily) bring species to the brink.

One thinks of the American settlers who languidly shot bison from moving trains, killing at least 60 million animals (though they had an even more dubious reason added to boredom for this slaughter—the government wanted bison extinct to starve out Native Americans).

Uniquely, we are a species that often destroys something for the sake of destruction or a desire to feel powerful. When I was a child I used to torture ants with a liquid blend of pesticide, toothpaste, milk, window cleaner, etc. I would watch them squirm and die for hours. I always felt bad when I did it, yet I still went ahead: this is where the view that life is entertainment leads us.

This is not to say that one can't be entertained at a zoo, but rather that such an experience should hopefully be complimented by education, awe, respect, and enlightenment. These are living and breathing beings, not pixels or stuffed bears. While western cultural humans may have a tradition of believing themselves vastly superior to all other forms of life, one would hope that seeing the breadth of a polar bear, the social organization of an ant colony, the unruffled beauty of an eagle, the gaze of a mountain gorilla, or the deadliness of a copperhead should be an avenue to question such beliefs, not reinforce them.

Zoo's effectiveness: analysis of a study

In 2007 AZA (Association of Zoos and Aquariums) published the findings of a survey that addressed many of the issues I have explored thus far. This survey—three years in the making—interviewed visitors from a total of twelve zoos and aquariums. They asked questions regarding educational experiences, conservation, and the place of zoos in society.

AZA, a respected organization, views their findings as proof that "visits to accredited zoos and aquariums prompt individuals to reconsider their role in environmental problems and conservation action, and to see themselves as part of the solution."

I am not surprised by their findings: zoos do produce a lot of good. The problem, however, is that instead of seeing gaps for improvement, the conclusions of the paper state that all is well and good. They're playing Pollyanna.

First, when AZA states that visiting zoos and aquariums causes reconsideration of environmental problems and conservation actions in the visitor and the belief that we—humans—are a part of the solution, it really means that 54 percent of visitors affirmed this. Fifty-four percent isn't bad, but it's hardly good. How do these zoos seriously feel about failing 46 percent of visitors? No one would view 54 percent literacy as admirable. While AZA contends its percentage is positive, I see it as proof that zoos are not doing enough—near enough—to change minds. I wish AZA had followed up this question by asking visitors to then list the concrete ways they learned during their visit in order to lessen their impact on the environment.

Another curious finding from AZA's assessment was the result of a test given to adults to see if their knowledge of ecological concepts improved by visiting the zoo. Only 10 percent of visitors were found to have better knowledge of ecology after visiting the zoo. AZA states that this is because zoos underestimated the knowledge of the visitors. If this is the case, should zoos not be rushing to provide more and better information? If the visitors have graduated from Ecology 101, shouldn't zoos step it up to Ecology 201?

For decades, zoos have stuck with the basics: name, habitat, a few sentences about behavior. Their conservation information is even more lacking. Inadequate information is not enough anymore, and this study proves that clearly. People are ready (and they must be) to come face to face with complex issues like climate change, biofuels, mass extinction, poverty, and conservation. But why just focus on the problems without solutions? You want to cut your carbon foot-print?: eat less red meat, buy less stuff, eat local foods, turn down your thermostat, purchase a vehicle that gets at least 45 miles-per-gallon, install solar, and vote your conscience. If I can list a few big things in one sentence, you'd think a zoo could do a lot more. Perhaps even offering courses and children's camps on how to live a sustainable life.

Ineffective zoos are immoral

When confronted with a caged animal, let us say the beautiful snow leopard, my brain sometimes flashes to Edmund Dantes from The Count of Monte Cristo, falsely imprisoned for fourteen years (incidentally about the lifespan of a snow leopard), leading to madness and a desperate escape. Just because these are not humans in prison does not mean that animals in the zoo do not "feel" their confinement.

Have you ever seen a polar bear pace back and forth, back and forth? That is called stereotypic behavior and has been compared to an insane man's ticks. Gorillas will pound on glass walls (and occasionally escape); tigers (who in the wild may have a territory of over 50 square miles) patrol the same small acre incessantly; primates may appear listless and withdrawn or overtly active from stimulants to keep zoo-goers happy; an eagle may have nothing more to do all day than sit on a single perch and defecate (most zoo birds no longer have the ability to fly, something that would instantly doom them in their natural habitat). No matter how much someone wants to dismiss the "intelligence" or "awareness" of these animals (and this is becoming increasingly difficult with every year of new research), one cannot argue against the fact that they are living a life to which they are not at all evolved. These are not tame animals; it took humans centuries, perhaps millennia, to turn the now extinct aurochs into the fatter, duller cattle we see on farms today: animals so far from their ancestors that they can only survive in managed environments. Putting wild species in a carefully managed, concrete environment is akin to locking a sane man in a madhouse.

If wild animals are not allowed to strike awe in the visitor and to be used as an opportunity to educate them about the decisions they (or their governments) make that affect their wild relatives, then their incarceration is not merely reasonless, but criminal. These animals are ambassadors for wilderness, for a biodiverse earth, for the planet as it is (or even as it was). This is not a role they have chosen, but one we have forced upon them. Zoos have a moral obligation to achieve the most good out of this sad state of affairs.

Final thoughts

An animal is worth more than a masterwork of art or an archeological treasure, simply because it lives. It breathes, it eats, it sleeps, it thinks, one day it will die; its true nature is impenetrable, because we can only view it through our own prejudices and limitations as humans.

I realize at times I probably sound terribly dour and that my ideas would suck all the fun out of any zoo experience, making it dim and serious. I am quite aware of this personal stuffiness: my wife likes to say that I am a zoo snob; I don't deny the possibility. But I do not mean that a zoo experience should not be enjoyable. Experiencing the zoo should never become any less fun, rather it should be given the added dimensions of awe and education, of respect and a higher purpose to save the vastness of life on this planet, and in turn save ourselves.

For me, I am a quiet zoo-goer. It is almost a spiritual experience for me. I stand before an animal—unique and beautiful—and I undergo a sense of meaning and rejuvenation. It is a strange thing to experience such emotions while the source of them is locked in a cage, but there it is. I understand those who can find no joy in a zoo and those who see zoos as cruel (inherently they are), and I would stand and protest with them, if not for the fact that all other species are in the midst of a devastating ecological crisis, and it may only be these caged ambassadors who make people wake up and act. The institution has responsibilities that should no longer be overlooked, but happily embraced.

Remember, the next time you visit the zoo, to stare an animal in the face and to know that the only reason this animal is where it is…is you. You and I and all of us are the reason these animals sit behind glass or bars; we are the reason only a fraction of their habitat remains; we are the reason they have been driven to almost nothing; and may very well—sooner than we can imagine—be extinct and gone, forever flung from living. What right do we have to do this? And what right do zoos have to exist, if not to show us our illusion of mastery,

our waste of creation, and our responsibility to make it right—
as right as it can be?

The zoo—if only it lived up to its purpose—could play a leading
role in the preservation of creation, the saving of life. I hope it
will take up its mantle, and leave behind the immaturities that
continue to plague it.

9

The end of the oceans: from bounty to empty

In the greatest novel about man's relationship with the denizens of the deep, Herman Melville devoted an entire chapter to the question of whether or not man could ever endanger a species of whale. His conclusion: "we account the whale immortal in his species, however perishable in his individuality." Herman Melville, of course, was wrong in this. Although an incredible surveyor of human nature, Melville was not as gifted in cetacean population dynamics. How could he be? Humans have long viewed the oceans as vast, bountiful, and ever-providing. Poet John Milton described the oceans as 'illimitable'; Shakespeare called them 'boundless' and 'infinite', and Lord Byron probably said it best, declaring that "Man marks the earth with ruin—his control / Stops with the shore."

The belief in this fallacy should not be surprising: until the 20th Century the nature of the ocean could only be determined by those abyssal inhabitants pulled up by line or net—imagine trying to comprehend the Congo rainforest from a few dead specimens brought to your doorstep. Early scientists were left to depend on speculation and imagination. Given this, why should the ocean not be illimitable? The ocean was not like a forest; one cannot cut down its trees. One cannot drain it like a lake. For much of history, in fact, it seemed reasonable that people could have little impact on the great blue. It was beyond us; it was impenetrable and inexhaustible; our impacts were like rocks thrown into waves: for one moment we would disturb the surface, but then the disturbance would vanish as though it had never been.

Today we know better. Industrial technologies, a throw-away global culture, vast sources of pollution, little-to-no management, climate change, and an explosive rise in the human population is exhausting the once inexhaustible.

"As we considered the cumulative effect of what humankind does to the oceans, the implications became far worse than we had individually realized," Alex Rogers, scientific director of International Program on the State of the Ocean (IPSO)'s, said after heading a recent panel of marine experts, who found that the oceans were being synergistically pummeled by multiple human impacts.

"We've sat in one forum and spoken to each other about what we're seeing, and we've ended up with a picture showing that almost right across the board we're seeing changes that are happening faster than we'd thought, or in ways that we didn't expect to see for hundreds of years," Rogers adds.

In just a generation or two, scientists have moved from understanding that we have the capacity to threaten marine species to realizing we have actually decimated whole underwater ecosystems. And then comes today: when scientists are having to face the fact that if we don't change our ways we could actually devastate the entire global ocean as we know it. This isn't just intuition, but is based on thousands of studies by the best marine experts.

A number of recent evaluations—including one by the IPSO panel and a review of marine research by Jeremy Jackson, director of the Scripps Center for Marine Biodiversity and Conservation at the University of California—have concluded that the life in the world's oceans is headed toward mass extinction. Yes, much has changed in the last 150 years: one could hardly imagine a more different prognosis from Herman Melville's.

"The purpose of [my] paper is to make clear just how dire the situation is and how rapidly things are getting worse," Jackson said in 2008. "It's a lot like the issue of climate change that we had ignored for so long. If anything, the situation in the oceans could be worse because we are so close to the precipice in many ways."

According to both papers, the oceans are facing three major issues: overfishing, pollution, and multiple impacts from climate change.

Fishing to death

When I recently asked a marine biologist, Claudio Campagna, what the greatest threats to the oceans were, he replied, "Simple: overfishing first, then overfishing. If we need a third threat: overfishing. Fourth to tenth: overfishing." Campagna is not alone: scientists and environmentalists have been fighting for years to rein in overfishing, but the stats tell a bleak story, one as short-sighted as commercial whaling at its gory height.

According to Jackson's paper, stocks of predatory fish—including tuna, salmon, cod, swordfish, and rays—have been diminished by 90 percent since the 1950s. In the North Atlantic, popular dinner items such as cod, pollock, and haddock—all predatory fish—have dropped by 89 percent in a century, leading to a near-total collapse in the fishing industry in this region. Both northern and southern bluefin tuna are considered Critically Endangered by the IUCN Red List, yet are still targeted by fishermen in a chaotic race to the last fish, and are only tepidly protected by a regulator that consistently eschews warnings for the vanishing species. In fact, five out of eight tuna species are currently listed as threatened with extinction, entirely due to overfishing.

In some cases, the decline of sharks has occurred even faster; a study in the Northwest Atlantic showed that population declined 40 to 89 percent in just fourteen years. While sharks are caught both for consumption and as bycatch, one of the greatest threats is a soup—that's right, a soup.

An increasingly popular Asian delicacy, shark-fin soup is exactly what its name suggests. Sharks are caught, their fins sawed off, and often the animals' bodies—sometimes still alive—are thrown back into the water (the shark meat is usually not even worth enough in monetary terms to store in the boat's freezer).

Shark finning alone is estimated to have killed an average of 38 million sharks per year between 1996 and 2000. According to the IUCN Red List, 32 percent of pelagic (open ocean) sharks and rays are threatened with extinction; in this case one would have to be an amphibian (40 percent) to have a gloomier future.

The widespread decline of marine predators has led to what is called a 'trophic cascade', wherein the loss of top predators causes population changes down through the food chain. As an example, Jackson points to the loss of sharks in the Northwest Atlantic. Here, their decline led to a rapid rise in the cownose rays (*Rhinoptera bonasus*), which were suddenly free from their only predator, big sharks. A population explosion of the ray to about forty million led to the collapse of clam fisheries, since the ray feeds on clams and oysters. A trophic cascade can run all the way down a food chain, leading to drops in zooplankton and rises in phytoplankton, changing an ecosystem entirely.

It's not just predatory fish that are targeted by fisheries around the world. Jackson writes that "oysters were the first invertebrates to suffer extreme depletion," adding that "the massive destruction of oyster reefs by dredging has permanently destroyed much of the formerly great habitat complexity of estuaries and coastal seas worldwide".

Oysters have suffered a global loss of 91 percent. The oyster population has been unable to recover due to habitat loss, nutrient pollution, and disease, Jackson notes.

Animals that are common bycatch for fisheries have suffered almost as much, and in some cases more, than the target fish. Bycatch—including non-target fish, sharks, seabirds, dolphins, marine turtles, and seals—are species that are caught and simply discarded as waste.

Of the seven marine turtle species, all are considered endangered to some degree, except the flatback turtle (*Natator depressus*), which lacks the necessary data. Three of the seven are Critically Endangered. Green turtles have plummeted from historical numbers of 90 million to approximately 300,000 today, a drop over 99 percent. The leatherback turtle has declined by two-thirds since 1980 in the most optimistic scenario.

A number of marine birds are also endangered because they are caught on longlines and drowned. A recent study estimated that even with tougher regulations and simple ways for fishermen to mitigate bird bycatch, around 300,000 seabirds are still killed annually.

Of 80 total marine species examined by Jackson, he notes that 91 percent are depleted, 31 percent have become rare, and 7 percent have gone extinct.

"Nowhere are there any substantial signs of recovery, despite belated conservation efforts, except for nominal increases in some highly protected birds and mammals," he writes.

The top three seafood consumers are (in order): Japan, China, and the US. In 2007 the US alone ate almost five billion pounds of seafood, 85 percent of which was imported. Of course, the five billion pounds does not include the amount of by-catch.

Following the collapse of target fish populations—and there have been many—industrial fisheries simply move on to other species until they too are decimated. A landmark study in 2008 predicted that if business-as-usual continues in the fishing industry, all wild fish stocks will collapse by 2048.

Having overfished much of the easily accessible parts of the oceans, industrial fisheries are now eyeing both the Arctic and

Antarctic. Melting sea ice in the Arctic is opening up once no-go areas to fisheries hungry for new markets. On the other side of the planet, fisheries are now targeting slow-growing Antarctica toothfish, dubbed Chilean seabass, in the Ross Sea. Known as 'The Last Ocean', the Ross Sea, only discovered in 1841, has remained entirely untouched by industry—until now.

"The Ross Sea is the last open ocean tract (i.e. not a reef) that still has an intact food web, much like what one would expect the 'Garden of Eden' to have been like," marine biologist David Ainley says. "All the 'fruits' are still there, ready to be picked."

And fisheries, mostly out of New Zealand, are moving in. Meanwhile, Ainley and others are scrambling to have the Ross Sea named a marine protected area before too much is lost.

Pollution: from dead zones to plastics

Dead zones, as the name implies, are regions where dissolved oxygen has fallen to such low levels that most marine species can no longer survive. Caused by an influx of nutrients, dead zones have created massive shifts in coastal ecosystems over the past fifty years. According to a recent World Resources Institute (WRI) study, these degraded regions have doubled every decade since 1960, reaching a record number of 415 in 2008.

Here's how a dead zone begins: nitrogen-based fertilizer, sewage, domesticated animal manure, or industrial runoff enters a coastal environment causing eutrophication—an increase in chemical nutrients. This surfeit of nutrients leads to massive algal blooms, which eventually die and are broken down by bacteria. The process uses-up the region's oxygen leading to hypoxia, essentially suffocating the area and pushing most species out.

Dead zones are usually seasonal, occurring every summer. But some sites have begun to show signs of becoming hypoxic over the long-term. These zones are not literally devoid of life; rather they have undergone massive population changes. Dead zones support "an extraordinary biomass of diverse microbes and jellyfish that may constitute the only surviving commercial fishery," Jackson writes, but little else survives. As such, dead zones have had large effects on fish yields and biodiversity in general.

As an example, Jackson writes that, "the iconic American example is the hypoxic dead zone that extends some 500 kilometers west of the Mississippi delta. The area of the hypoxic zone has doubled in the past 20 years to 20,000 square kilometers." Runoff into the Mississippi, especially of nitrogen fertilizer, is behind this massive and infamous dead zone.

This is not the way it used to be: "analyses of the geochemistry and mineralogy of cores shows that hypoxic conditions were uncommon before the 1950s," writes Jackson. The only way to stop such dead zones is to regulate the pollutants causing them.

Other types of pollution, such as plastic trash, have also had a major impact on wildlife. Plastic is known to ensnare marine mammals and birds, often leading to injury, sometimes even death. Leatherback sea turtles often mistake plastic bags for jellyfish, a behavior that can eventually kill the deep-divers.

New research is also showing that tiny plastic particles in marine ecosystems are more nefarious than expected. Plastic particles absorb chemicals such as flame retardants and synthetic musks, which are then consumed by marine life. These chemicals have been found as far abroad as the polar seas. Other research has found that plastics decompose in the oceans much faster than expected, releasing potentially toxic substances.

The oceans have long been human dumping grounds, but not long ago most materials thrown in were made of wood, glass, or steel; they rotted or wore down. Now, with the advent of industrial chemicals, modern fertilizers, and plastics, pollution is changing the very character of the oceans. The largest symbol of this is the great plastic trash island that bobs in the Pacific Ocean, swaying like a vast blanket of bubbles just beneath the surface; the trash pile has garnered creative names such as the Great Pacific Garbage Patch and the Plastic Trash Vortex. Reportedly, the 'island' expands to twice the size of Texas.

'Uncontrolled experiments' in play

As bad as overfishing and pollution are, many of their impacts are generally, at least cursorily, known. However, according to Jackson, the effects of climate change on the ocean are an "uncontrolled experiment".

Carbon dioxide, emitted by human activities, is entering the ocean at a rate not seen since the last marine mass extinction around 55 million years ago. Increased carbon sequestered in the oceans leads to acidification (lower pH levels), which imperils the world's coral reefs, threatens algae species, and may doom iconic animals, like the clownfish. The full impacts of today's acidification are not yet known, but 55 million years ago half of marine species vanished.

The first marine causality of the increase of carbon dioxide is the ocean's most biodiverse ecosystem: coral reefs. Ocean acidification reduces the capacity of reef-building organisms to form the calcium carbon skeletons that serve as their structural basis. At the same time, higher temperatures cause reefs to lose the tiny symbiotic organisms that provide them with sustenance and are essential to their survival.

Jackson writes that "just 15 years ago, many coral reef scientists still referred to coral reefs as pristine" but a recent report from the IUCN warned that one-third of coral reefs are now threatened with extinction. In less than three decades coral reef populations worldwide have fallen by half.

"It is difficult to imagine how corals will be able to survive or reefs persist if the rise in CO2 continues unabated," Jackson says.

Citing particularly extreme cases, Jackson writes that Caribbean coral cover has plunged from 55 percent to five percent in about 25 years. Seventy percent of coral species in Florida that were common in 1880 are common no longer, while 40 percent of these are actually Endangered or Critically Endangered.

"Today many scientists believe that the cumulative forces of overfishing, pollution, and climate change are so great that coral reefs may virtually disappear within a few decades," Jackson writes.

In addition, climate change is melting Arctic sea ice and Greenland glaciers faster than anticipated, risking not only rising sea levels, but the possibility of methane release from underwater deposits. The full impacts of global warming on the polar seas are as yet unknown, but species dependent on sea ice—such as polar bears and walruses—may not be able to adapt to a new ice-free Arctic.

Mass extinctions

"The findings are shocking," Alex Rogers said of the IPSO's report, which makes the case that all of these impacts together are not allowing marine ecosystems time to recover, putting the world's oceans on track for a mass extinction event.

Five mass extinctions have hammered the Earth in the past half billion years, and many scientists suggest we are seeing the signs of a sixth, although usually they point to the destruction of the world's rainforests as proof, not the degradation of the oceans.

However, the IPSO panel found that past mass extinctions of marine life included three signs: increased hypoxia or low oxygen levels, rising temperatures, and ocean acidification. As we have seen, all three of these are occurring today due to human impacts, but that's not all—overexploitation of marine life is adding an additional toll.

Reviewing current trends and statistics, Jackson agrees with the ISPO's bleak prognosis for the oceans. Overfishing will eventually create environments that are almost wholly devoid of commercial and predatory species, leaving only "small, opportunistic species," he says. Dead zones will continue to increase in number and size due to agricultural and industrial nutrient runoff, while a warming ocean and continued greenhouse gas emissions will worsen acidification. Eventually, mass extinction could occur leading to "profound loss of animal and plant biodiversity". In this future ocean, says Jackson, "microbes will reign supreme".

The future ocean—and how to stop it from happening

The ocean of the 21st Century is nothing like that of the early 20th Century, and even less like that of Melville's time. We have so imperiled its ecosystems that the ocean can no longer be regarded as a reliable source of food for the future, threatening livelihoods—especially in poor nations—around the world. It is a place under siege, facing the possibility of mass death.

"These predictions will undoubtedly appear extreme, but it is difficult to imagine how such changes will not come to pass without fundamental changes in human behavior," Jackson writes. "Moreover, as we have seen, all of these trends have actually been measured to a limited degree in the past few decades […] Some may say that it is irresponsible to make such predictions pending further detailed study to be sure of every point. However, we will never be certain about every detail, and it would be irresponsible to remain silent in the face of what we already know."

Sobering date and awful predictions don't necessarily mean it is impossible to change the fate of oceans.

"The challenges for the future of the ocean are vast, but unlike previous generations, we know what now needs to happen. The time to protect the blue heart of our planet is now, today and urgent," says Dan Laffoley, Marine Chair of IUCN's World Commission on Protected Areas and co-author of the IPSO report.

So, how do we do it?

"The only way to deal with it is in segments; the only way to keep one's sanity and try to achieve real success is to carve out sectors of the problem that can be addressed in effective terms and get on it as quickly as possible," says Jackson.

First and foremost, according to IPSO researchers: immediately cut greenhouse gas emissions. Jackson calls this, "the greatest challenge to humanity today," a statement agreed upon by many scientists and world leaders. While global society has proven sluggish when it comes to cutting emissions, there is still time to halt the worst impacts of climate change if we move swiftly and decisively.

Regarding the impact of fisheries, Jackson says that the issue is not one of knowledge but rather implementation.

"The only thing standing in the way of sustainable fisheries and aquaculture is the lack of political will and the greed of special interests," he writes, noting that many good laws and management programs are already in existence, but are not enforced.

The IPSO recommends restructuring industrial fisheries for longterm sustainability, including shutting fisheries that are not sustainable; establishing more marine protected areas; tackling pollution and nutrient run-off; and reducing oil, gas, and mining in the oceans. The scientists say that the 'precautionary principle' must be used in terms of oceanic impacts, in other words society shouldn't proceed with activities unless they are proven to be largely safe for marine ecosystems. Finally, researchers say the UN General Assembly must more effectively govern and regulate activities in the high seas, which are currently beyond any national jurisdiction.

Noting an undiminished demand for seafood, Jackson writes, "wild fisheries cannot possibly sustain increasing global demand regardless of how well they are managed," and suggests that "industrial-scale aquaculture of species low on the food chain is the only viable alternative. But this in turn will require strong new regulation to prevent harmful ecosystem consequences."

To gain control of the nutrient pollution causing eutrophication, Jackson suggests rolling back fertilizer subsidies and proposes a tax on fertilizer use. He believes such action would impose "only modest decreases in food production and increased costs". However given rising food prices and global population growth that shows no sign of slowing down, such changes may be untenable for society. Still, losses in agricultural could be made up for in gains in local fisheries as many of the world's poor depend entirely on wild fish for protein.

In addition, Jackson states that using less fertilizer would reduce greenhouse emissions. Here, a shift towards more organic practices could aid both terrestrial and marine biodiversity.

"The challenges of bringing these threats under control are enormously complex and will require fundamental changes [but] very significant actions could begin right away without further scientific research or technological innovation," says Jackson, who has introduced a new method of explaining the vulnerability of the ocean's various ecosystems, one that could be very easily understood by the public-at-large.

"Just as we say that leatherback turtles are critically endangered, I looked at entire ecosystems as if they were a species," he says.

Jackson labels coral reefs, coastal areas and estuaries as Critically Endangered. He believes that continental shelves are Endangered, and the open ocean, Vulnerable.

While Jackson laments that "the problems appear so overwhelming that many are ready to write-off coral reefs and all of the other marine life that will be drastically affected," he believes that local conservation actions to protect the oceans from other threats could allow species time to develop resistance against the effects of rising CO_2 levels. He notes that the atolls of the Central Pacific show relatively healthy coral populations despite climate change, probably because these reefs do not face other perils, such as over-fishing, nutrient or toxic pollution, and habitat destruction.

Some progress is being made, albeit haltingly. Marine Protected Areas (MPAs), a relatively new concept, have been spreading fast around the globe; currently over 6,000 MPAs have been established. However, there is far to go as these MPAs only cover 1.17 percent of the world's oceans and only 0.08 percent are under strict protection.

More recently, sharks have received periodic good news. A number of nations have begun creating 'shark reserves' which ban shark hunting and finning. In addition, shark fin soup has been banned outright in a number of US states, most notably California. Also in the U.S., regulators have recently cut catch-rates of the tiny fish menhaden, described by cultural historian, H. Bruce Franklin, as the 'most important fish in the sea' for its role as prey for big fish, seabirds, and marine mammals. This was reported as a landmark decision that surprisingly pushed back against years of lobbying.

Sure, these are small movements compared to the immensity of the problem, but Jackson says such regional and local measures are hugely important.

"Local conservation measures may help to buy time for marine ecosystems until we bring the rise of greenhouse gases under more effective control," Jackson says, adding that while the scale of these problems is immense, "We have to begin somewhere".

10

Language and conservation: why words matter

The words we choose matter. Benjamin Lee Whorf, an influential American linguist, theorized that the language we use directly impacts our perception. Whorf wrote: "language shapes the way we think, and determines what we can think about." This is not as revolutionary as it sounds: any psychologist can tell you that language, and its structure, has conscious and subconscious power. Taken simply, if a parent tells a child that it is "better" than its peers, how will it view itself in relation to its community? Likewise, if a parent calls a child "fat," it doesn't take a doctorate to predict what the child will see in a mirror.

The power of words goes beyond human relationships. For example, if we are told a forest is "dangerous," "scary" or "wasteland," we will view it as such: a place that must be tamed or destroyed. This can also happen in the reverse. In the 1990s environmentalists concerned with logging in a particularly diverse British Columbian rainforest renamed the forest in question the "Great Bear Rainforest" after the ecosystem's population of grizzlies, black bears, and a rare strain of white-colored black bears. It had previously been called the "mid and north coast timber supply area." One name focused on what made the forest unique (and thereby beautiful), the other on the material value of destroying the forest. Eventually, environmentalists won a partial victory, saving one-third of the forest from any logging whatsoever.

I was recently reminded of the power of words in conservation—even innocently spoken ones—during a trip to southern Africa. Over two weeks my wife and I visited protected areas in Zimbabwe and Botswana; the animals we encountered and the scenes we were fortunate enough to witness proved so wondrous that I have a difficult time describing them—at least in any way that accurately depicts the experience. But one aspect of our travels troubled me as we left.

The first instance was at Chobe National Park in Botswana. Not far from the river that gives the park its name, our guide referred to the impalas we were watching as "Africa's McDonalds." The reason for this, he explained—after he didn't get the requisite chuckles he expected—was because impalas have black marks on their rump, outlined by white, and when their tail is positioned just so the marks appear to make an "M". It's not a great likeness of the ubiquitous McDonalds logo, but somehow the antelope attained the nickname—also apparently because they are "fast food" for lions—and now can't shake it off.

I was a little bothered that the guide didn't take that moment to tell us something about the impala's natural history, such as its ability to jump nine meters (thirty feet), or the fact that it is active during both the day and the night, or that its social structure is flexible enough to change group structures depending on food availability.

But it was a small thing, all in all, so I didn't think about it again until we visited a private wildlife park in Zimbabwe, and our guide told us the same thing. Only this guide took it one step further: every time we would see an impala he would boisterously call out "McDonaaaaalds!" instead of referring to it by its common name, impala, or, I even wondered, why not its scientific name Aepyceros melampus? I would've loved to hear someone—anyone—pronounce that.

As our visit wore on, I realized this was becoming a trend. Zebras instead of being zebras were "donkeys in pajamas!" and worst of all was the name give to the waterbuck (*Kobus ellipsiprymnus*). This antelope has a white circular mark on its hindquarters, and so the guide called it, "toilet-seat buck!"—his voice ringing out over the savannah. Yet to me the waterbuck is an especially attractive large antelope with the males' horns sweeping up like two facing crescent moons.

Now, this got me thinking: if what we choose to name something matters, if it shapes our perception and our very thoughts, then what did it mean to visitors that these animals, which they may only see in the wild once in their lives, were referred to as "McDonalds," "donkeys in pj's," or "toilet-seat bucks"?

Seeing animals in the wild, watching the way they interact with their natural environment should be an experience of awe and profound respect. It should be a moment to remember, treasure, and share. But if one's guide is calling the animals nicknames that are silly or even demeaning, how can one really see these animals for what they are: unique living beings inhabiting this bewildering and prodigious world with us.

Both the reserve in Zimbabwe and the park in Botswana exist, at least in part, for the conservation of species, yet how could conservation be a success if we demean the species we are asking people to help conserve?

We spent a part of our visit in the Zimbabwe park with a French family with two young boys. I wondered what they would remember best from their trip to the bush. Would it be their encounter with animals not in a zoo, but in a wild space, or those ringing nicknames in the air?

This train of thought led me to other phrases common in African lingo. In Africa, parks and reserves are called "game parks." This is leftover language from the time when the majority of these places were literally for the purpose of "game," i.e. white people shooting animals with rifles. While there are still true "game parks" in Africa (where people can pay to shoot pretty much any species they like) the majority of reserves are places for the conservation of wildlife. Why not then call these parks what they are: "wildlife parks" instead of "game parks"?

Just think about the difference in these two names: small but important. When I think of "game animals" I think of animals that live simply to be shot for human pleasure, trophy hunting as it were. When I think of wildlife, I see many species interacting; I see full ecosystems with individuals being born, living, reproducing, and dying. Sure, calling such places 'game parks' may be a cute echo of the past, but is it worth retaining the image it presents—whether conscious or subconscious?

Along the same vein is the propensity for Africans—and tourists—to refer to the "Big Five." Like "game parks" this is an archaic reference to when wealthy foreigners visited the bush to shoot animals instead of view them. The Big Five literally refers to the five most difficult animals to kill: the elephant, lion, African buffalo, leopard, and rhino. Yet despite the context surrounding this phrase, it has come also to mean the five animals that tourists most want to see. Not because these are necessarily the species an individual tourist most hopes to see (birders, for example, will be disappointed by the Big Five), but because it's what tourists are told—over and over and over again—that they should want to see. Unfortunately this establishes pressure on the guides to continuously look for the Big Five. The more of the Big Five they can show, the "better job" they have done.

But why the Big Five? Why should African parks and guides be chained to a list that only made sense when people walked out into the bush with a firearm? Why not the Big Ten, such as elephant, lion, African buffalo, leopard, rhino, giraffe, hippo, hyena, Nile crocodile, and cheetah? Or better yet why not ditch the list altogether and just enjoy the wildlife that happens by you, big or small, the object of past hunters or not. Compared to the open African plains, in the Amazon rainforest, one sees so little compared that one is grateful for any sighting big or small: bird, mammal, amphibian, or insect, brief or lone. One is simply happy to have a glimpse of the life that hides in the shadows of endless green. I wish tourists would bring the same come-what-may attitude to Africa as they bring to the Amazon. Such an attitude allows both tourists and guides to relax.

Once our guide in Zimbabwe realized that my wife and I were engrossed and interested in the animals' ecology—and not their nicknames—he actually dropped his veneer and began to explain passionately about the animals we were seeing. I thought then that perhaps calling the animals by nicknames was not cultural, but simply a way in the trade to keep bored tourists interested. I imagine most safari guides would rather share their love and respect of the African wilderness with you, instead of having to play some clownish role to keep you 'entertained'.

But isn't this emphasis on entertainment dangerous in itself? Life forms did not evolve on Earth for billions of years only to entertain us. To put it another way, they are not "games." For if we value biodiversity and nature as merely for our entertainment then we will only care about conserving species and environments that we find especially "likeable." We, however, know that natural ecosystems are worth far more than entertainment. Along with providing essential services for our own survival—clean water, food production, pollination, carbon sequestration, medicine, and others—they also have deep spiritual, cultural, and psychological worth. Not to mention the moral beliefs underlying all conservation efforts: all living breathing animals deserve deference.

A trip to Africa to see its wildlife should be an experience that goes well beyond entertainment: it should be educational, enlightening, moving, spiritual, and ultimately transformative. When a guide refers to species by silly nicknames one can't help but feel that the guides place little value on their own wildlife, though I suspect this is not the case; they feel pressured by a world that values flashy entertainment more than reality. Instead, I hope guides will share both their knowledge and awe of their nation's wild lands, instilling respect for the creatures tourists are viewing and impressing upon the visitors the importance of conservation efforts for the survival of many of Earth's inhabitants.

In the end, few people would devote time, energy, or funds to save "the toilet-seat buck" or the "McDonalds antelope," but it is worth everything to know that in our world a group of impala graze on the dewy foliage, or a bold male waterbuck shelters itself in the trees, and a zebra's distinct stripes still flash against an African sunrise.

Words matter, let's put them to better use.

11

Saving the world's weirdest mammal

Imagine a drunk, waddling rodent with venomous snake-fangs and an ability to chirp like a dolphin, and you'll have some sense of the little-known, 76-million-year-old solenodon. After long neglect by conservation groups and scientists, the solenodon is enjoying a renaissance in both research and conservation efforts. Native to the Caribbean island of Hispaniola—with Haiti on one side and the Dominican Republic on the other—the Hispaniolan solenodon (*Solenodon paradoxus*) has recently been discovered to still survive in Haiti and be more abundant than expected in the Dominican Republic. Now conservationists are working to save the species that not long ago appeared fated for extinction.

Introducing an odd fellow: the solenodon

There are few animals in all the world stranger than the Hispaniolan solenodon. The species can perhaps be best described as a multi-colored plump rat with the long dangling nose of an elephant shrew; its eyes are tiny pinpricks, while its feet have long gnarled toes and nails that appear in desperate need of trimming. Something about the animal makes it look old and cantankerous, like an insectivorous Yoda, while its implausibility makes it appear a work of the human imagination rather than nature's, a chimera courtesy of Hieronymus Bosch perhaps. But the Hispaniolan solenodon is no flight of fancy.

"I could not quite believe it the first time I held a solenodon; I was in utter awe of this mesmerizing mammal. [...] They have a long flexible snout, which is all down to the fact that it is joined to the skull by a unique ball-and-socket joint. This makes it look as if the snout is almost independent to the rest of the animal. You can't help but feel fascinated by the snout and inevitably it does make you smile," says Dr. Jose Nunez-Mino, the Project Manager for the Last Survivors. The Last Survivors is a new conservation program devoted to the solenodon and the hutia, another bizarre Caribbean mammal.

The solenodon renaissance kicked off in 2007 when researchers from EDGE, a program of the Zoological Society of London (ZSL), rediscovered a small population of Hispaniolan solenodons in Haiti. Prior to this, it was believed the solenodon might have been extirpated from the impoverished country. A year later, scientists in the Dominican Republic captured some of the first footage ever of a living solenodon. Suddenly, this odd little bloke, so long ignored, was appearing on new sites across the world.

Dr. Samuel Turvey, a member of the EDGE research team who rediscovered the species in Haiti, explains that solenodons have a special hold on evolutionary scientists: "[they] constitute an ancient mammal lineage that diverged from all other living mammals around 76 million years ago, during the time of the dinosaurs".

The Hispaniolan solenodon has only one living relative, the Cuban solenodon, which Turvey describes as "only distantly related". Both species are often referred to as "living fossils" since they are essentially windows into the early mammals of the Cretaceous.

The solenodon also has a hidden surprise.

"They are the only living mammal species that are able to inject venom through specially modified teeth, similar to the way that snakes inject venom—a very unusual adaptation for a mammal!" exclaims Turvey. While there are other venomous mammals, including two species of shrews and the male duckbill platypus, they are capable only of passively conveying venom: shrews' venom resides in their saliva and duckbill platypuses possess a poisonous claw on their hind leg. But the solenodon secretes venom through grooved incisors like a viper. This adaptation, says Nunez-Mino, gave the solenodon its name: "the word 'solenodon' derives from the Greek for channeled tooth."

Greater observations of the solenodon have also led to new interest in the animal's vocalizations, which Nunez-Mino describes as "a series of clicks and high-pitched whistles." While no one yet knows what these vocalizations are for, it hasn't stopped researchers from speculating.

"There has been some suggestion that these [vocalizations] may be implicated in echolocation, but as far as I know there has been no conclusive work in this area. We have managed to make some initial crude recordings of the solenodon which have roused a lot of interest with scientists that work in this area," Nunez-Mino says.

Echolocation is used by a number of mammals, from bats to dolphins, to locate food or for navigation purposes. However, the only terrestrial mammals that are known to use echolocation are shrews and tenrecs.

In spite of its unique place in the kingdom of life, the Hispaniolan solenodon faces immense pressures. Its forest habitat has been invaded by alien predators and degraded by humans, allowing only small populations to hold on in forest fragments. Before European colonization of Hispaniola, it is believed that the solenodon had no natural predators. Its slow and clumsy gait—hardly useful for evading predators—is cited as evidence for this.

"[Hispaniola was] never colonized by true carnivores," Turvey explains, "so solenodons probably represented the top mammalian 'predators' of these unusual island ecosystems before human arrival, although they are generalist insectivores rather than really carnivorous."

However, once Europeans arrived the island became overrun with dogs, cats, and the Asian mongoose, all of which prey heavily on the island's endemic species, including the solenodon. People have also been known to kill and eat the creatures. Given centuries of onslaught, it is really quite surprising the solenodon survived at all.

In fact, this was the second upheaval where the solenodon beat the odds. Researchers have found that before humans arrived in the Caribbean—around 4,000 years ago—the islands were home to 120 unique mammals (not including bats), from 200-pound ground sloths to a bear-sized rodent, and from endemic monkeys to massive numbers of the Caribbean monk seal. Today, only 15 of the 120 mammals survive: an extinction rate of over 85 percent.

Not surprisingly, the appearance of invasive species, compounded by on-going human encroachment and habitat degradation, pushed the solenodons—one of the last 15—to the verge of extinction. By the 1990s a couple populations persisted in the Dominican Republic, but Haiti's only population of solenodons was predicted to have only 10-20 years left before it vanished. While the bleak prognosis was due largely to the amount of pressure on the solenodon, it also reflected the general laxity of the conservation community toward species that don't have the requisite popularity with the public. This is a trend EDGE is working to overcome.

"So far solenodons have been sorely neglected by conservationists," Turvey says, "many of whom have probably never even heard of them."

Many animals are known publicly simply for the bizarreness—the duckbill platypus, the narwhal, and the naked mole rat—so why not the solenodon? The animal tells a long and deep story about the early history of mammalian evolution, yet it has reigned in obscurity. Beyond these merits to science, Nunez-Mino says a live solenodon has a charming quality that is impossible to resist.

"When handled properly they are remarkably docile and relaxed which makes it very easy to observe them in the hand. [...] All in all I think it is fair to describe solenodon as amazingly cute. They have a toy-like quality about them which is reinforced by their very small eyes and their cumbersome walk which is more of a side-to-side waddle."

Rediscovery in Haiti

In April, 2007, Dr. Turvey and colleagues spent eleven days in the Massif de la Hotte region of Haiti, hoping to ascertain if any solenodons still survived or if the country had lost one of its natural treasures. This mountainous region was the last place solenodons had been confirmed; previous researchers outlined an area of solenodon habitat in the Massif de la Hotte of only about eight to ten square kilometers. Turvey had experience with tracking down lost species: a year earlier he'd been witness to the extinction of the baiji.

But, in this case, the survey uncovered good news. The scientists' interviews with subsistence farmers and villagers and the subsequent discovery of three dead solenodons— one of which had been eaten by a farmer—confirmed that the solenodon still roams Haiti. In fact, the researchers believe that the species' range may be even larger than it was a decade ago: they found evidence that the solenodons occupied lower elevations than expected and could even survive in largely degraded habitat. In a paper in Oryx announcing their results, the researchers hypothesize that a widespread culling of dogs in the region may have saved the solenodons from extinction and even allowed them to expand their tiny range.

The re-discovery of the Haitian population of solenodons proved important for an additional reason. The authors stressed that preservation of solenodon habitat and conservation measures would not only aid the solenodon but other endemic and endangered species, including Hispaniola's only endemic rodent, the hutia, which is classified as vulnerable by the IUCN, and the gray-crowned palm-tanager, listed as Near Threatened. The Massif de la Hotte region may also be ripe for new discoveries: while visiting for just eleven days the researchers made the first sighting of an indigo bunting in Haiti and recorded the island's first yellow-headed blackbird.

Despite this wealth of biodiversity, conservation in Haiti faces many hurdles.

"Haiti is the poorest country in the Western Hemisphere, and obviously the ongoing humanitarian crisis [from the 2010 earthquake] has meant that there have been few national resources available for conservation or environmental work," Turvey said. "So far there are only a couple of sites in the entire country that have been awarded national protected status. The Massif de la Hotte is home to a large number of unique endemic species restricted to this small mountain region, but although it contains one of Haiti's few national parks, and has been identified as a globally significant region by the Alliance for Zero Extinction (AZE), there still is little concerted conservation activity even here."

The earthquake has only worsened matters.

"Last year's devastating earthquake in Port-au-Prince has obviously led to tremendous and ongoing problems across all sectors of Haitian society, and has understandably slowed down environmental conservation efforts in the country. The development of our field project in Haiti has inevitably been slowed down," explains Turvey. "In the aftermath of the earthquake, many Haitians fled Port-au-Prince to return to their home communities in rural regions, which has placed additional stresses on the last remaining forests of the Massif de la Hotte."

However Turvey adds that conservation efforts in the Massif de la Hotte are progressing again, including 3-year funding from the UK's Darwin Initiative.

"We are now preparing a full-scale survey of all of the remaining forest fragments in these mountains to better understand the distribution of land mammals, bats, birds and amphibians in different fragments—to prioritize these forests for urgent conservation attention," Turvey says.

The solenodons of the Dominican Republic

Around the same time that the EDGE team was surveying the Massif de la Hotte in Haiti, conservation work concerning solenodons was beginning on the other side of the island.
In the summer of 2008, conservationists with the Durrell Wildlife Conservation Trust (DWCT) and the Ornithological Society of Hispaniola, set out to survey solenodons in the Dominican Republic. The field team was surprised by how successfully they were able to find solenodons, given the animal's presumed scarcity.

"During one month of intensive trapping effort one individual was caught in a live-trap, providing a valuable DNA sample and some very rare film footage of the solenodon after the animal was released," Richard Young, a conservation biologist with DWCT who worked on the survey.

The DWCT, created by the popular author and honored naturalist Gerald Durrell, focuses much of its attention "on conserving vulnerable communities of endemic animals which make such a valuable contribution to global biodiversity," according to Young. Like EDGE it has a history of working with species and places that haven't gained the attention of the larger conservation community. Organizations like these—that buck the trend of focusing only on popular animals—have meant the difference between extinction and rejuvenation for the solenodon.

DWCT's initial survey was the start of a new conservation program, The Last Survivors, now headed by Nunez-Mino. According to Young, the idea was to "enable the long-term conservation of the Hispaniolan solenodon by conducting large scale surveys to assess its population status and a field study in order to identify the main human-driven threats to its survival."

To date, The Last Survivors has conducted surveys across the Dominican Republic, including in Sierra de Bahoruco, Jaragua, Punta Cana, Isla Catalina and Parque del Est. It has also expanded widely to include important research.

"The project is now also supporting a PhD student who is radio-tracking solenodons to better understand how they use forest and agricultural environments, as well as three MSc students who have studied other aspects of solenodon ecology and field techniques over the past couple of years," Turvey explains, adding that "ongoing research into the recent fossil record in Hispaniola is also providing new insights into changing patterns of solenodon abundance over time, and what this means for their conservation today."

Nunez-Mino adds that a part of the work by The Last Survivors has been to raise awareness about the species both locally and around the world. One of his biggest surprises was arriving in the Dominican Republic only to discover that few people had ever heard of the solenodon.

"Once you explain that they are found nowhere else on earth, people generally show an immense sense of pride in them," he says. An 18-year-old has even started a business of selling hand-made stuffed solenodons.

The final step for the program will be to "design and implement an effective conservation action plan", which will be meant to keep the species safe—and monitored—indefinitely.

The future of the solenodon

After fending for itself in an increasingly desperate situation, the solenodon has made a number of important friends in just a few years. Along with EDGE and DWCT, the solenodon has found champions in the Ornithological Society of Hispaniola, the Audubon Society of Haiti, Zoo Dom (the Dominican Republic's National Zoo), the Go Wild BBC Wildlife Fund, Punta Cana Resort & Club's ecological foundation, and the Darwin Initiative. The Last Survivors, which is a collaborative effort by a number of these organizations, is devoted to conserving not only the Hispaniolan solenodon, but also other surviving mammals in the Caribbean.

The Cuban solenodon, unfortunately, has not received the same support as the Hispaniola. Once thought entirely extinct, the Cuban solenodon is believed to be hanging on by a thread.

"It is now only encountered very rarely, unfortunately often when animals are killed by dogs," Turvey explains. "We hope that the field techniques that we have developed for surveying the Hispaniolan solenodon can also be used for monitoring solenodons in Cuba, as part of a wider-scale Last Survivors project."

While the solenodons' future remains precarious, the Last Survivors project will be vital if they are to survive.

A final mystery remains. In 2001 biologist Jose Alberto Ottenwalder suggested that the solenodons of Haiti may be distinct enough from those in the Dominican Republic to represent a subspecies; Ottenwalder went ahead and named it Solenodon paradoxus woodi. Others have even suggested the solenodons in Haiti could be a distinct species, providing even greater urgency to the conservation of the more threatened Haitian population.

Such debate is not new to solenodons. The taxonomy between the Hispaniolan and the Cuban solenodon is also under discussion: some believe they should not share the same genus since the two species are separated by an astounding 25 million years—around the first appearance of apes in the world.

Hopefully the answers to these age-old questions should soon be known.

"The Last Survivors project has been collecting samples from solenodons found across Hispaniola—including both historical museum specimens and animals encountered during fieldwork—and we are now in the process of carrying out genetic analysis of these samples to better understand the evolutionary relationships between different solenodon populations across the island. Our findings will then be used to inform conservation management of different populations, depending on how evolutionarily distinct they are found to be," explains Turvey.

When asked about their hope for the future of the solenodon, both Turvey and Young proved cautiously optimistic.

Noting their extreme scarcity and the number of threats they face, Turvey sees hope in the mammal's ability to survive: "solenodons seem to be tenacious little animals in many ways, as they have somehow managed to survive in the West Indies when over 100 other land mammal species have died out in the region as a result of human activities."

Young says that the species has a chance "given some good conservation science and planning and if effective partnerships between national and international partners can be built, conserving this species is possible but actions are needed urgently."

Both scientists agree that without active conservation the solenodon would likely go extinct. There is little doubt that if this is allowed to happen, the world will suffer the loss of one of its most special inhabitants: a hodge-podge, motley little monster, wonderful enough to make Dr. Seuss envious of nature's creativity.

12

Shifting baselines: forgetting the lost

Visiting an exhibition of historical maps at the New York Public Library, I was taken aback to realize the city I had lived in for nearly a year had once been a dense green forest, surfeited with Mid-Atlantic plants and animals, and the Lenape people. To me, New York City was a manic mega-metropolis, an artificial land so far removed from the natural world that when a red hawk showed up in Central Park in the 1990s, residents went wild with amazement and still talked about it in hushed awe in 2006. No, New York City was built wholly out of concrete and simply did not exist before the Gilded Age. The idea of indigenous people, deer unaccustomed to traffic, and beaver once roaming the same ground I now stomped along with 8 million other Homo sapiens—stemming from practically every corner of the Earth—made me doubt my current reality. I had a difficult time conceiving of Walt Whitman's New York City, let alone the Lenape people's.

Looking back, the surprising thing was not that trees used to stand where skyscrapers now stood (that should have been obvious), but the bizarre fact that I had such a hard time believing it. My experience—of being unable to conceive how an environment has changed over generations—has become known to scientists as 'shifting baselines'.

"The shifting baseline syndrome is the situation in which over time knowledge is lost about the state of the natural world, because people don't perceive changes that are actually taking place. In this way, people's perceptions of change are out of kilter with the actual changes taking place in the environment," E.J. Milner-Gulland, with Imperial College London, says.

In other words, due to short life spans and faulty memories, humans have a poor conception of how much of the natural world has been degraded by our actions. Our "baselines" shift with every generation, and even in the life of an individual. What we see as pristine nature our ancestors would view as hopelessly degraded, and what we see as degraded our children will consider "natural." New York City is an extreme, but apt, example, since over generations the knowledge of what used to be was so lost that encountering it today—in a map exhibit of all places—seems like science fiction.

Scientists first elucidated the concept of shifting baselines in 1995 while exploring how urban children perceived nature. In the same year, marine biologist Daniel Pauly coined the term "shifting baselines." Since then the idea of humans perceiving nature inaccurately, through knowledge gaps, has sunk into the conservation world, helping researchers understand more fully our relationship with the environment. But while many were drawn to the theory, it had yet to be tested in a scientific manner: were people actually undergoing shifting baselines or was something else occurring? For the first time two recent papers—one in Conservation Letters by researchers at Imperial College London and the other in Conservation Biology by scientists with the EDGE program at the Zoological Society of London (ZSL)—put shifting baselines to the test.

As the Conservation Letters paper's authors write, "one of the biggest current issues in assessing the implications of [shifting baselines syndrome] is the lack of empirical evidence that it occurs."

Generational and personal amnesia: birds of Yorkshire

In their Conservation Letters study, researchers at Imperial College London tested two different types of shifting baselines: generational and personal amnesia. The use of the word 'amnesia' is important because any experience of shifting baselines involves a loss of information without being aware of any loss, a kind of amnesia.

"Generational amnesia is when knowledge is not passed down from generation to generation. For example, people may think of as 'pristine' wilderness the wild places that they experienced during their childhood, but with every generation this baseline becomes more and more degraded," Eleanor Milner-Gulland, one of the researchers, explains.

For example, if legendary conservationist John Muir returned to Northern California today there is no doubt that he would believe much of the wilderness he loved to be terribly,

154

hopelessly altered: dams, roads, endless sprawl, etc. However, a native Californian may see parts of the landscape as perfectly natural; national parks are often viewed by Americans as the emblem of nature—even with roads running through them clogged with traffic, artificial barriers that cut ecosystems, and people, lots and lots of people. This type of altered perception of nature occurs with each succeeding generation until it is entirely forgotten that even a place like New York City was once wild.

Personal amnesia is quite different and perhaps even more insidious. Rather than occurring at every generation, personal amnesia happens quicker, during a single individual's lifetime.

"Personal amnesia is when people forget how things used to be during the course of their own lives; for example they may not remember that things which are rarely sighted now were once common," says Milner-Gulland. In this case, the individual actually 'updates' the changes as they occur, so that the change (along with the past) is forgotten and the new state becomes the baseline.

But how do you test such amnesia? Supplied with concrete data of bird population changes in Yorkshire County, England, Milner-Gulland and colleagues interviewed 50 rural villagers regarding their perception of changes in the surrounding birdlife populations. Interviewees were asked what the most common birds in Yorkshire were today versus 20 years ago. Surprisingly—or not, depending on your view of human nature—researchers received a wide variety of answers.

The scientists found evidence of generational amnesia, since "older people were more accurate at naming the commonest birds 20 years ago than younger people were," Milner-Gulland explains. "This is not because older people are just better at naming common birds, because there was no difference in accuracy for the present-day birds. So, it suggests that there is a difference between generations in understanding of how the typical bird fauna of the village has changed over time."

In addition researchers found that over one-third of participants had a static view of bird species in Yorkshire. In other words, they chose the same species as common both twenty years ago and today—even though that was not the case.

"These people tended to think that the bird fauna has always been how it is now, rather than naming those birds which were more common in the past. This suggests that they were updating their perceptions over time without realizing it," Milner-Gulland says, pointing to concrete evidence of "personal amnesia."

Researchers could find no underlying reason why certain people had a static view of bird populations while others noticed change—accurately or inaccurately. But they had achieved their goal, concluding that: "this study provides the best evidence to date for generational and personal amnesia."

Even big animals quickly forgotten

It's not only bird populations in an English county that are forgotten; another study—this one in Conservation Biology—found that people forget large charismatic mammals too, even those that once served a mythic role.

The Yangtze River dolphin (*Lipotes vexillifer*), known as the baiji, was declared extinct in 2006 after a survey down the polluted, industrialized river failed to find a single individual. Years later, the large charismatic marine mammal is not only 'likely extinct', but in danger of being forgotten, according to a surprising study "Rapidly Shifting Baselines in Yangtze Fishing Communities and Local Memory of Extinct Species".

Lead author of the study, Dr. Samuel Turvey with the Zoological Society of London (ZSL)'s program EDGE, was a member of the original expedition in 2006. He returned to the Yangtze in 2008 to interview locals about their knowledge of the baiji and other vanishing megafauna in the river, including the Chinese paddlefish (*Polyodon spathula*), possibly the world's largest freshwater fish, with some individuals recorded at 21 feet (7 meters) long. In these interviews Turvey and his team also found clear evidence of communities undergoing rapid shifting baselines syndrome.

"Communities can forget about changes to the state of the environment during the recent past, if older community members don't talk to younger people about different species or ecological conditions that used to occur in their local region," Turvey explains. "These shifts in community perception typically mean that the true level of human impact on the environment is underestimated, or even not appreciated at all, since the original environmental 'baseline' has been forgotten."

Turvey and his team felt that the Yangtze River, one of the world's most degraded freshwater habitats, would provide a more-than-suitable place to test the theory in the field. But even they were surprised by the extent to which once-important species were forgotten.

"Our data from the Yangtze shows that, in certain cultural environments at least, local communities will immediately start to forget about the existence of even large, charismatic species as soon as these species stop being encountered on a fairly regular basis," Turvey says.

The team interviewed 599 participants ranging in age from 22 to 90. While the majority of participants had heard of the baiji (89.7 percent) and the Chinese paddlefish (66.2 percent), the researchers found that the one thing that linked those who had never heard of the species was youth.

"Younger informants were less likely to know what either species was, despite being prompted with photographic cue cards, appropriate local names, and verbal descriptions," the authors write. For example, 23 percent of participants who had begun fishing after 1996 had never even heard of the baiji.

"Often we would interview old fishermen who regaled us with stories about the best way to catch paddlefish with long-lines, or told us recipes about how to cook a baiji and what it tasted like, and then we would talk to a 30- or 40-year old fisherman sitting a couple of meters away in the same fishing village who had absolutely no idea what these species were or what we were talking about," Turvey told mongabay.com, adding that, "it is particularly surprising because paddlefish (the largest freshwater fish in the world!) used to be culturally and economically important until the 1980s, and the baiji was the focus of myths and legends across the Yangtze region."

It has been pretty well established that the baiji is extinct. Even if a few individuals survive it is highly unlikely that under current conditions in the river—massive dams, susceptibility to bycatch, illegal electric-fishing, pollution, collisions with ships—they could persist in the longterm.

Less is known about the Chinese paddlefish. The massive fish has not been the target of conservation efforts or publicity campaigns like the baiji, despite its importance to local fishermen as a food source. The Chinese paddlefish began to decline precipitously in the 1970s due to overfishing; the construction of several major dams added to its problems, and in the 1980s the population collapsed. While the International Union for the Conservation of Nature (IUCN) hasn't evaluated the Chinese paddlefish population since 1996, a recent local survey failed to find a single individual. Some now believe the species, like the baiji, is either extinct or very soon will be.

"I have to say that sadly I don't hold out much hope for the survival of the paddlefish, even in the short term," explains Turvey. "Although it's possible that there might still be a tiny remnant population of paddlefish left in the Yangtze, any survivors downstream of the Gezhouba and Three Gorges dams are cut off from their spawning grounds, so they cannot reproduce. Fishing efforts and the wider-scale industrialization of the Yangtze are also continuing to intensify, in particular through an increase in destructive electro-fishing."

The great fish, a record holder, is being forgotten by the young generation faster than the baiji. A stunning 70 percent of participants who had begun fishing after 1996 had never heard of a Chinese paddlefish, proving the old adage, out of sight, out of mind.

Turvey says that the world has let the species go without even a whimper.

"It must also be recognized that, shamefully, there has been extremely little conservation interest ever paid to this magnificent species; at least the baiji was the focus of a lot of conservation discussion, whereas the plight of the paddlefish didn't even receive that level of recognition."

A complete lack of conservation efforts probably explains, at least in part, why the Chinese paddlefish has been forgotten even quicker than the baiji.

Shifting baselines in a vanishing ecosystem

Considering that the Yangtze river ecosystem may have lost two key species in less than a decade, and possesses a high number of Critically Endangered species according to the IUCN—the Chinese alligator (*Alligator sinensis*), the Yangtze sturgeon (*Acipenser dabryanus*), and the Yangtze soft-shell turtle (*Rafetus swinhoei*)—one has to ask: is this an ecosystem that will soon be forgotten entirely?

"The Yangtze ecosystem—a vast river drainage once home to hundreds of unique endemic species—is now undeniably one of the world's most damaged, degraded habitats, and it is extremely depressing to try to carry out conservation projects there," says Turvey. "The problem is especially acute because the region continues to experience tremendous industrial development associated with China's escalating economic growth, and it is also home to a huge number of low-income communities that depend upon the river for resources and livelihoods."

One year after the baiji was declared likely extinct, a report by China's official State Environmental Protection Administration (SEPA) found that 30 percent of the Yangtze river's tributaries are "seriously polluted" while 600 kilometers of the river's water is in "critical condition." Yet development continues: China is currently proposing to build another dam on the river, which according to researchers would impact the river's only fish reserve and one of the last places where the Chinese paddlefish is thought to survive.

The degradation of the river and the loss of species have also impacted the region's fishermen. In their survey, Turvey and his team found that over 90 percent of the fishermen didn't want their children to become fishermen. Important commercial species, such as Reeves' shad and the Yangtze pufferfish, have both undergone population collapses. According to SEPA the river's annual harvest of fish has dropped 77 percent from the 1950s to the 1990s, leaving fishermen struggling to make a living and resorting to more drastic methods, such as electro-fishing, a practice putting the final nail in the coffin for some species.

"Under such conditions, it is often hard to see how conservation successes can be achieved—is it just a case of banging your head against a wall as you watch species slide irreversibly towards extinction? But how can we allow ourselves to ignore this kind of environmental problem?" asks Turvey.

Currently the Yangtze finless porpoise (*Neophocaena phocaenoides asiaeorientalis*), a freshwater subspecies of the finless porpoise, is estimated to have a population of no more than 2,000 individuals. The Chinese alligator is on the brink in the wild, but survives in captivity. The Yangtze soft-shell turtle, which may also be the world's largest, could already be gone from the Yangtze, although a wild individual was recently found in Vietnam. Researchers are trying to breed two of the last captive turtles, but one of the turtles is over 80 years old, and the other over 100. Turvey says that for species like these, captive breeding is likely to be the only way to save them in the long run, although as the turtles' prove even captive breeding is not fail-proof.

"As for many of the Yangtze's other threatened species, unfortunately very little is still known even about their status or necessary conservation measures," Turvey explains. For example, the Critically Endangered Yangtze sturgeon hasn't been assessed by the IUCN for over a decade.

In the end shifting baselines may apply not only to single species, but to an entire ecosystem. One day the inhabitants of the Yangtze River may be shocked to hear about all the 'great beasts' that once inhabited their river, as shocked, say, as an inhabitant of New York City is to learn that Times Square, a paean to global consumerism, was once a red maple swamp.

Implications for conservation

Turvey believes their findings have large significance for conservation efforts in China and beyond.

The study proves that "although local ecological knowledge is a highly important source of information for making conservation decisions and recommendations, there are also major problems with relying solely on information provided by local people when trying to reconstruct past changes to the environment," he says.

When people's views of pristine nature shift with every generation, or even in an individual life, it makes conservation work an uphill battle. How can environmentalists convince people that the environment is degraded when they don't see it that way?

"If we don't realize what we are losing we stand the risk of sleepwalking through the destruction of the natural world without taking action to remedy the situation," Milner-Gulland points out.

This is the fundamental difficulty behind shifting baselines syndrome: how to make conservation important when people do not see the loss. For example, in the western United States wolves have been locally extinct for so long that no one remembers when they were plentiful. As far as local communities are concerned, wolves are not a part of the natural environment, therefore this personal perception of nature—of it being "natural" not to include wolves—may add to resistance to wolf reintroductions in the region, and could hamper other proposed reintroductions, such as the campaign to create a free-ranging bison herd in the American prairie.

The problem is especially exacerbated when scientific data is not available regarding past conditions of an ecosystem, unlike wolf or bison in the United States. Unfortunately, hard data is often difficult to come by, especially for environmental conditions generations ago. Yet, as Milner-Gulland points out, scientists are becoming increasingly creative in finding data regarding past conditions that may no longer be remembered.

"One author, Julian Caldecott, used school meal records from remote village schools to reconstruct wild pig migrations in Borneo. There are many authors now using historical records and archeological remains, for example in charting the changes in fish stock compositions in the North Sea over thousands of years. Other people use contemporary accounts from eye-witnesses, while still others use scientific methods like pollen analysis, which can go back far beyond written accounts." Milner-Gulland adds that, "the important issues involve recognizing and accounting for sources of bias in the records that you use."

Even given the scientific data, other questions still remain.

"There is a huge difficulty in setting baselines for conservationists to work towards, either in measuring change or in setting targets for restoration. Where do we set the baseline—100 years ago, pre-industrial times, say 400 years ago, or where?" Milner-Gulland says. The question really becomes what will society accept when one tries to restore a degraded world?

Despite all the difficulties posed by shifting baseline syndrome, Turvey also points to a possible upside to the research: "If communities forget about vanishing species very quickly, then maybe our findings could also suggest that reports of supposedly extinct species might turn out to be true."

Knowledge is the first step

Knowledge of the shifting baselines problem, however, could go a long way toward remedying how people view their environment.

"If we can identify the factors that make people's perceptions more or less in line with reality, we can put conservation measures in place to keep them aligned. That's one step away from people actually taking action of course, but it's the first step towards it," Milner-Gulland says.

Milner-Gulland encourages conservation organizations to begin taking shifting baseline syndrome into account when working in education and community efforts.

"For example if there was an issue in an area with generational amnesia, it might be worth targeting conservation interventions to engage with older people, and enlisting their help in telling the younger generation how things were only a few decades ago," Milner-Gulland suggests. "This is not that common an approach in conservation, which often explicitly targets the young. If even the older generation has lost this knowledge, then conservationists could use books or photos to engage people with how their environment has changed."

In addition, simply intervening with scientific data may be enough to counteract at least some of the effects.

"If the issue is with personal amnesia, just talking to people and triggering their memories about how things were, perhaps with the aid of props like photos or old specimens, will help them to ensure that their perceptions of change are accurate," Milner-Gulland says.

Since shifting baselines is a young theory, Milner-Gulland sees a need for further inquiry in order to truly understand the effects of the theory on conservation and environmental action.

"In terms of research, we need a lot of studies, in both the developed and developing world, that help us to understand how people's perceptions of environmental problems vary with their characteristics (e.g. their age or their exposure to the target of our conservation concern)," Milner Gulland says. "I think that the whole area of how people perceive environmental change, and how these perceptions align with real change, is an exciting field of study, which still only has a handful of studies. If we are to act effectively to conserve the environment, we first need to make sure that people (and society in general) accurately perceive the problem. Without this, interventions to conserve nature may have unintended consequences, or at best be less influential than they could be."

There are obviously limits to 'correcting' a degraded natural world. So long as humans reign, New York City will likely never again be a deciduous forest, but small victories are important too: in 2007, a beaver returned unaided to the Big Apple, making a dam on the Bronx River after being absent at least 200 years.

13

Gone: extinction over the past decade

Sometimes conservation fails. Funds, support, and time may just not be on the side of the conservationist and, despite last-ditch efforts, a species slips into extinction. More often, however, a species vanishes in part because it has not received targeted help. Neglect can be as big a threat as invasive species and overexploitation.

In the end—and, make no mistake, for most of the species highlighted below, this is the end—no one can say with any certainty how many species went extinct over the last decade (2000-2009). Because no one knows if the world's species number 3 million or 30 million, it is impossible to guess how many known species—let alone unknown—have gone extinct recently. Species in tropical forests and the world's oceans are notoriously under-surveyed, leaving gaping holes where species can vanish, taking all of their secrets—even knowledge of their existence—with them.

It is also difficult to know when a species is truly gone. There have been numerous cases of species reappearing after they were thought extinct for decades, sometimes even centuries. In May 2011, a red-crested tree rat (*Santamartamys rufodorsalis*) showed up at a rainforest lodge in Colombia, surprising volunteers with a local conservation group. The problem was the red-crested tree rat was supposed to be extinct: it had not been seen since 1898. This is the main reason why, officially, species are usually not considered 'extinct' until ample time passes without a sighting, for example, fifty years. The red-crested tree rat, however, is an exception, and with many biologists and conservationists warning we are in the midst of a human-caused mass extinction, it is important to recognize likely vanished species before we know for certain they are gone, if only to remind ourselves of our own impact and our conservation failures.

Scientists have announced a number of likely extinctions (as well as extinctions in the wild) over the past ten years. Here we look at fourteen such extinctions.

The Yangtze River, extinction hotspot

The most publicized extinction over the past decade is the baiji, also known as the Yangtze River dolphin (*Lipotes vexillifer*).

While the baiji's evolution goes back 20 million years, it couldn't survive China's great development boom and subsequent environmental crisis. A combination of dams, boat traffic, pollution, overfishing, and electro-fishing led to the species' demise, giving the baiji the dubious title of the first (known) marine mammal to go extinct since the 1950s. The dolphin was a character in Chinese myths and was colloquially known as the 'Yangtze River Goddess', but none of this could save it from an economic and industrial juggernaut.

But the baiji is not alone; another denizen of Yangtze may have vanished recently. A recent survey of the Chinese paddlefish (*Polyodon spathula*), one of the world's largest freshwater fishes, failed to find even a single individual. While researchers believe the fish probably still survives, no one knows for certain—and no one knows how long it can persist in such a highly degraded habitat.

The Chinese paddlefish has been decimated due to the same reasons as the baiji: dams, traffic, and pollution, although overfishing is probably the biggest cause. The last confirmed paddlefish was killed by illegal fishing in 2007.

Unless China acts quickly other species of the once-fabled Yangtze will not survive the next decade, including the finless porpoise (*Neophocaena phocaenoides asiaeorientalis*), the Yangtze sturgeon (*Acipenser dabryanus*), and the Chinese alligator (*Alligator sinensis*) (although the alligator survives in large numbers in captivity).

A lesser Hawaii

Like the Yangtze River system, the Hawaiian Islands—famous for unique birdlife—are an extinction hotspot. In this case, extinctions have been occurring at high rates for centuries, ever since the Polynesians first arrived. And they are ongoing.

In 2002 the 'Alala (*Corvus hawaiiensis*), also known as the Hawaiian crow, went extinct in the wild when the last two known individuals vanished. The bird suffered from a number of threats, including habitat loss, introduced rats, mongooses, and disease, as well as illegal collecting. The 'Alala was not the first: fossils show that four other crows have already gone extinct in Hawaii. But the 'Alala had long held a special place in Hawaiian culture: native Hawaiians considered the crow a household god.

Fortunately the last word has yet to be written for the 'Alala since over fifty individuals survive in captivity and the possibility of reintroduction is being discussed.

Another of Hawaii's birds is not so lucky: the Po'ouli (*Melamprosops phaeosoma*) or black-faced honeycreeper went extinct in 2004. Unknown to science until the 1970s, the shy bird was endemic to the island of Maui alone. By the beginning of the decade only three individuals were known to survive. One died in captivity in 2004; the other two have not been seen since.

While other Po'oulu could survive, no one knows for sure and it seems unlikely that a healthy breeding population will be found. Unlike the 'Alala, reintroduction of the Po'oulu is an impossibility.

These birds are only the most recent representatives of a long decline in Hawaiian native avifauna: half of Hawaii's 140 historically-recorded endemic birds are gone forever.

Back from the dead (for a moment)

In addition to the baiji, the last decade saw the extinction of a number of other large mammals.

In a most ignoble end, the world's last Pyrenean ibex (*Capra pyrenaica pyrenaica*) was killed by a falling tree on January 6th, 2000. A subspecies of the Iberian ibex, the Pyrenean ibex once roamed across the Pyrenees in both France and Spain, but spent most of the Twentieth Century on the verge of extinction. Although no smoking gun has been determined for the extinction, hypotheses include disease, climate change, poaching, inbreeding, and low fertility.

Nine years after its extinction, the species returned for a moment: a clone of the subspecies was born but died from lung failure after a few breaths. The species was the first extinct animal to be successfully (sort of) cloned.

Rhinos no more

The rhinoceros is one of the world's most threatened big mammals: of the five remaining species, three are Critically Endangered, one is Endangered, and only the white rhino appears secure for the time being from extinction. One by one the ongoing pressures of habitat loss, poaching for horns, and population scarcity are taking out the world's rhinos.

The western black rhinoceros (*Diceros bicornis longipes*)—a subspecies of the black rhino—met its end during this decade. Hunted relentlessly for its horn, the rhino went from thousands historically to just ten individuals hanging on in Cameroon. By 2006, however, a survey found that none of the rhinos remained.

Three years later and the last Vietnamese rhino (*Rhinoceros sondaicus annamiticus*)—a subspecies of the Javan rhino—was killed by a poacher's bullet to the leg. Its death leaves the Javan rhino species with only around 40 individuals surviving in a single park on its namesake island.

Rhino poaching is on the rise, fueled by the mistaken belief in Eastern Asia that rhino horns contain medicinal properties. Unless action is taken quickly to stop the illegal wildlife trade, it is not improbable that the next decade will see more rhino extinctions.

Little flying mammals' last take-off

Bats represent the largest family of mammals; with over 1,200 known species bats make up about one-fifth of the world's mammals. But unlike their mostly non-flying cousins, bats rarely receive intensive conservation care, at least not from big NGOs. Bats remain misunderstood by much of the public, seen as objects of fear and loathing, instead of as indispensible seed-dispersers and pest-eaters.

The end of this decade may have been the end of one bat species: the Christmas Island pipistrelle (*Pipistrellus murrayi*). Weighing in at just three grams, this tiny bat's demise has been meticulously recorded: in 1994 there were 100 bats, in 2006 there were 54 bats, in February 2009 there were 20 bats, in August only a single bat was recorded, and none have been seen since.

Scientists simply don't know what killed off the micro-bat. They lived in a protected area and had ample food. Could it have been an invasive species, some unknown disease, pollution, or some cause not-yet-guessed-at? Anything is possible, but we may never know.

The decade to come could be especially bad for the world's bats, as a disease known as white nose syndrome is sweeping across North America, killing millions. The disease is so virulent it is pushing once common bats to scarcity.

Amphibian Armageddon

As difficult as it may be to be a bat, being an amphibian is worse. There is likely no class of species more imperiled than amphibians: devastated by a still-mysterious disease, the chytrid fungus, and hit by climate change, habitat loss, and pollution, this particularly sensitive family is in the midst of an extinction crisis. Around 40 percent of the world's amphibians are considered threatened by the IUCN Red List, with almost 500 species listed as Critically Endangered.

The Kihansi spray toad (*Nectophrynoides asperginis*) vanished from its home in the middle of the decade. Living adjacent to a waterfall and gorge in Tanzania, the toad survived on only two hectares of land. Then the World Bank built a dam in the area, changing the flow of the waterfall and degrading the environment. Surveys found fewer and fewer toads until, eventually, they found none.

Fortunately, a population of Kihansi spray toads still survives in captivity in the U.S. Reintroduction would only be possible, however, if their native habitat could be made to support the toads again.

The Panamanian golden frog (*Atelopus zeteki*) —a beautiful black and gold species—also likely vanished from the wild during the last years of the decade. A national symbol of Panama, the frog was devastated by the chytrid fungus and habitat destruction. Like the Kihansi spray toad, the Panamanian golden frog survives in captivity, but its future is hardly secure.

These are but a small representation: it's possible 150 species of amphibians have gone extinct since 1980; however, few of these have been confirmed. With climate change scenarios growing increasingly dire, rampant deforestation, continuing pollution, low levels of public awareness, and no cure yet to the chytrid fungus, it's unlikely the 2010s will be any better for amphibians. However a few conservation groups--Amphibian Ark and SAVE THE FROGS!—are focusing entirely on turning the tide of amphibian Armageddon.

The vanished forgotten

While extinctions of mammals, birds, and amphibians garner the most media attention (in that order), invertebrates and plants are vanishing just as frequently.

Sometime between the end of the 1990s and during the beginning of this decade, the last Aldabra banded snail (*Rhachistia aldabrae*) succumbed to desiccation. Little-known, this snail was endemic to the Aldabra atoll. Since the snail hibernates during dry periods, less rainfall over the Aldabra atoll due to global warming likely spelled its doom.

Another invertebrate lost to climate change is the European land leech (*Xerobdella lecomtei*). A survey between 2000-2005 found only a single living European land leech. The researchers believe that a rise of three degrees Celsius during the summertime has doomed the leech, which is adapted specifically to the cold.

Climate-sensitive species from polar bears to pikas, from frogs to coral reefs are facing an uphill battle to survive in our warmer world. Extinctions due to climate change will likely become even more common in the next decade.

Invertebrates are not the only little-known and often-overlooked species. Plant extinctions—or discoveries for that matter—rarely make the news. In December 2003, the last Saint Helena olive (*Nesiota elliptica*) died in captivity. Prior to this, the species had vanished from the wild in 1994.

Endemic to Saint Helena Island, the Saint Helena olive perished from deforestation and the introduction of alien species like goats. No one knows how many plant species fell into oblivion during 2000-2009, but with high rates of rainforest destruction in many nations, it is likely that a large number of plants—many unknown to science—were lost in the last ten years.

Goodbye and maybe hope?: The last known wild Spix's macaw (*Cyanopsitta spixii*) disappeared from Brazil in 2000. This beautiful macaw was battered by habitat loss and trapping for the pet trade. While it's possible some wild macaws remain, more surveys are necessary. Still, even if no wild Spix's macaws survive, the species has a chance thanks to conservation efforts.

A small population of Spix's macaw survives in captivity and there has been recent success with reproduction efforts, especially at Al Wabra Wildlife Preserve which has bred 21 birds since 2004. In addition, Al Wabra has purchased Spix's macaw habitat in Brazil for possible future reintroduction.

Of the fourteen species noted here, Spix's Macaw probably has the most hope of surviving the next ten years. For the unfortunate others, this decade was their last stand.

14

The anaconda and the fer-de-lance: one day on Suriname's jungle coast

A travel essay

Although I would like to write "the day began and ended with snakes," the serpents merely enclosed its most important events like bookends. The first snake was straight out of mythology—both of the north and the south. The second was less mythical, more diminutive, but far more terrifying in the life-and-death way that truly matters.

My wife and I had traveled to Suriname because I was attending a conference for the Association of Tropical Biology as a journalist. Since we were making the trip down to a country few Americans had ever heard of, let alone visited—several times we were misinformed by know-it-alls that we were not in fact going to South America, but Africa—we decided to make an exploratory trip of it. As nature enthusiasts and David Attenborough addicts, we signed on for two weeks of volunteering with marine turtles, including the world's largest, the leatherback, on Suriname's coast.

But it wasn't the leatherback sea turtle that dominated my thoughts before traveling: it was snakes, specifically killer snakes. My boss, who spends about a quarter of every year traveling the tropics, had recently told me of a close call in Belize with two fer-de-lance. Given my nervous, and at times obsessive disposition, it was only a matter of time before I started scouting the Internet about the region's most lethal snakes. And, as it turned out, the deadliest of all was the hypersensitive fer-de-lance—the same species whose fangs just missed my boss. While I was excited to meet a leatherback marine turtle—something we were guaranteed—I was even more convinced I would step on a fer-de-lance and perish in some melodramatic, tropical kind of way, widowing my wife and leaving my boss without a reporter. In saner moments, I reassured myself with just how unlikely it is to find a snake in a rainforest.

But by the time this narrative begins—following four flights, a truck drive across the eastern half of Suriname, and a four-hour boat ride north along the Marowijne River—it was too late to turn back.

Pointing excitedly, our guides—from a nearby Amerindian tribe—turned the boat around and steered it toward a small beach on the edge of a deep mangrove forest. For a brief moment we thought we had arrived at our destination, but were confused by the lack of evidence of human habitation and couldn't clarify with our guides, since we didn't share the same language. Eventually, however, one word repeated by the guides in their thick accents made its way into our consciousness—anaconda.

The first snake of that day is perhaps most easily conjured up from Byzantine artworks of St. George standing over the dragon. Here was the dragon those westerners imagined— only halfway across the world and bigger. The anaconda rested on a small beach protruding from a dense mangrove forest, a shadowy place where thousands of species live in quiet obscurity.

The length didn't shock me as much as the girth. It was less palm tree, more oak. The deceased was engorged, greatly so, giving us not the width of a living Anaconda, but a dead one, ballooned from gasses released after decomposition. Still, in the bloated corpse we could see the full capacity of the anaconda to stretch its body to fit the prey. I used to think: anaconda— world's largest snake. But now I think: anaconda—I could fit comfortably inside.

The guides told us later they thought the beast measured six meters long, around nineteen and a half feet. I didn't doubt it. There is a lot of debate surrounding the maximum size of the world's longest snake. Such snakes are notoriously difficult to measure, especially in the wild: try to get a garter snake to lie straight enough for an accurate measurement, let alone an anaconda. Generally, an adult anaconda measures around 17-20 feet, with maximums being set at 23-25 feet. While some sightings have claimed snakes up to a hundred feet (almost certainly fabrications), there have been reports from somewhat reputable sources of anacondas reaching around 36 feet, all from over fifty years ago—such animals are often referred to as Giant Anacondas, and today receive more attention from cryptozoologists than Amazonian herpetologists.

But there was something tragic about this anaconda that set it apart, even if it wasn't the biggest ever recorded. As though St. George—tall, grand, and handsome—had fought this Devil's snake himself with a broad sword, the anaconda was headless. Yes, its head was no longer attached to its neck: in fact it was nowhere to be seen.

It's impossible to know why this animal—enormous, daunting, but glimmering and graceful—should be slaughtered and left so. Not for eating, since only its head was purloined. Sometimes anacondas are killed for their skin, but again why leave the body to rot—because rotten it surely was? Was it a jaguar? Americas' largest cat has been known to prey on anacondas—usually by crushing their skull with its teeth—and leave the body. But the clean cut suffered by the snake—as though a guillotine had come all the way from revolutionary France—made the jaguar an impossibility.

I could turn up nothing else on such an odd occurrence, which leaves me to speculate that perhaps the head had been taken for sale as a souvenir to some tourist. It's amazing how many visitors are bold enough to wander through the amazing virtues of the Amazon, but still buy a wild macaw in the illegal pet trade or eat beef locally connected to forest destruction. People will spend thousands of dollars to travel to a different continent to see a leatherback turtle, but then when informed—at a local restaurant—that one of the most threatening activities to the great species' future existence is shrimp fishing, lo and behold they order the shrimp. The capacity of humans to live with moral disconnect is peerless. I do it every day in America: cars, planes, baths, and books. I am more to blame than whoever beheaded the snake.

So, here was our first bookend: a mystery wrapped in the enigmatic relationship between humans and the world's other inhabitants. A relationship that, whether we realize it or not, spreads like a spider web across us all, connecting us to the poor farmer in Cameroon, the indigenous woman in Sarawak, the politician from Rondônia, and the banker on Wall Street. And from us it links everything from diatoms to elephants, redwoods to dung beetles.

A short way down the river from the anaconda's final resting place, we came on the first of two native villages. At first I thought this was—again—our home for the next two weeks. In point of fact, it was just a place to get gas, though it turned out there was none to be had. This stop was fortunate for us, however, as we got to ramble along the beach and I got my first sight of the black vulture. I pointed to the big bird and asked one of 'the guys' (this would become the customary term for the men working with us at the lodge) what it was and he said slowly: 'stink bird'. I think he was surprised that I would ask about what to him was an innocuous pestering bird.

The vulture took to the air from the beach and followed our boat; in another moment of overcoming linguistic barriers, the men called out in bits of English to me: "It—following—you!" They laughed. I feigned smelling my armpits, which made them laugh harder, though awkwardly. One of the guys in the boat had been kind enough to shimmy up a beach-side tree—with the same ease one imagines a magical Santa Claus goes up a chimney in more northern latitudes—to pick a few mangoes. As we watched the mangroves pass by, my wife and I peeled and ate the best mangoes we ever had.

Twenty minutes later we stopped in a second village. Four bronze-colored boys swam just off the beach, while a young one sat on the shore with a shirt on, naked from the waist down. Their mother, shoulder-deep in the water, held onto one of the moored boats. While one of 'the guys' ran off to get gas, we watched these boys with interest. A part of me wanted to say 'hello' or make some gesture, though I shied away from that. Why interrupt the boys in their reverie? It was clear they were showing off for the unacknowledged strangers— as children do everywhere; they did underwater handstands, they somersaulted, and smiled as though on stage. A brawl began as two of the brothers fought over I-can't-remember-what. The younger, fey throughout, laughed and laughed as his older, larger brother (whom the guys referred to as 'the fat one') repeatedly attempted to drown him, launching himself onto his brother like a killer whale on a seal. While the one pounced and the other dodged, the third caught an underwater sea creature in a coke bottle and at the behest of the guys proceeded to show it to us, shyly. The tiny anthropod scuttled around its prison like a trapped djinn. The mother beamed, and we couldn't help but beam as well at these young boys-being-boys: undulled by television, video games, cell phones, and the endless sensory overload of the world we'd left behind.

From here it was a relatively short trip, a half hour or so, to the Warana Lodge—our place of marooning for two weeks. When I saw it finally, I knew it couldn't be anything else but our temporary home. The lodge rests in what appears to be impossible in our contemporary world: seemingly endless miles of undeveloped beach.

As the boat pulled up we saw a group of elderly white women straight out of the American suburbs standing on the beach. It was not a sight we expected. Another white woman, in her twenties and sporting a tan that had nothing unnatural about it, was digging in the ground in would become her characteristic attire: a two piece. Liz, an American marine biology student working with the leatherbacks, was our consistent contact who spoke English. The elderly women from all over the US were volunteering with Elderhostel; they would only be around a couple days, but we would get to know Liz well. However at this point, we just grabbed our things and were guided to our quarters: a cement room with two bunk beds, a little smaller than a college dorm.

We spent the remaining daylight hours accustoming ourselves to our tiny space, the equatorial sun, and our diet for the next two weeks, which incorporated three choices: rice and beans, pasta with canned red sauce, or peanut butter and jelly sandwiches. The program didn't provide food for its volunteers, so we spent a mad hour in the capital, Paramaribo, purchasing what we hoped would be food enough for the two weeks.

In the late afternoon, once the sun was in decline, we took a walk along the beach. The thin strip of sand, a barrier between the jungle and the ocean, appeared like a little snake on the map in the lodge. Walking on it, however, was a different story. The smooth wet sand, constantly shifted by the tides, gave way to a second buffer zone of weedy dunes and tall grassland that suddenly ended against a wall of sixty-foot high trees. There was no transition: the landscape went from waist-high grass and dunes to the ecosystem that covers nearly all of Suriname: tropical lowland rainforest. The change was so sharp, it seemed almost man-made but, of course, man had little impact here.

The beach itself proved another matter altogether. Despite lying completely undeveloped, despite being protected as a nature reserve, despite being in a nearly unknown nation with few funds, hordes of trash invaded the turtles' beach: cheap plastic sandals, water bottles, lighters, white plastic utensils, juice cartons, butter containers, gasoline containers, Styrofoam to-go containers, tubes of toothpaste and toothbrushes, plastic bags of every color, beer bottles, prescribed medication still in its pop-out sheet, a screwdriver, and SUN laundry detergent— which is advertised all the way from Paramaribo to Galibi on roadway hand-painted signs. Coca-Cola shareholders would be pleased to note it is by far the most represented brand on the beach, both in bottles and bottle caps. The entire Galibi beach is a free advertisement for the brown saccharine liquid.

Plastic outweighed glass three to one on the beach, which is noteworthy, since glass eventually breaks down and causes little harm to oceanic wildlife, but plastic is a cancer to ocean species—marine turtles especially. Once, in the Caribbean Island of Tobago, a scuba-diver told me how her friend in Thailand did a post-mortem on a green turtle and found eighty cigarette butts and twenty plastic bags. The turtle had died of constipation; it simply couldn't remove those alien items from its intestines. Leatherbacks are known for mistaking plastic bags for the jellyfish they primarily feed upon. Enough bags and a leatherback will succumb. Scientists have identified 267 oceanic species that plastic trash harms, including nearly half of all sea birds and marine mammals.

But where did all this trash come from? It's not like thousands of tourists descended on this beach: the turtles coming up to lay their eggs every night outnumbered the people. Some of the trash certainly came in from the open sea: boats were not infrequent in the area. But most of it probably came downriver on the Marowijne River from the villages we passed and the town of Albina further down. Surrounded by the river and jungle, it is unlikely the Amerindian villages had any regular trash pick-ups and Albina was a small, but bustling town. I could imagine plastic drifting downriver from there like clouds in the sky.

During our stay, one of the older American ladies suggested we should go to the native villages and give them a good talking-to about throwing trash in the river. I felt a few misgivings about such a plan. I have two rules when traveling. Number one: tourists should never tell locals how to live—especially if the tourist is American. Second, following a similar creed, Americans have no leverage, whatsoever, in lecturing another nation regarding environmental issues. As citizens of one of the world's most gluttonous countries anything we say—anything at all—is hypocrisy.

I imagined stalwart Americans—five old ladies, their guide, a young married couple, and a marine biologist—marching up to the Amerindian village like cowboys packing heat, and delivering a lecture entitled "Stop Throwing Things in the River (Though We Don't Actually Know If You Are)." Then, we Americans would be happy and proud of our self-righteous 'commitment to save the environment' as we take a gas-powered boat back to Albina, where a truck would pick us up to take us to Paramaribo, where we would dine at one of the finest restaurants in the city eating shrimp and steak and drinking until there was no space left in our bodies for more, and then we would ride groggily in a taxi to the airport where we would embark on several different planes to our cushy lives in California, Iowa, Florida, Arkansas, free of poverty and necessity, but full of consumerism and distraction. Needless to say, the suggestion was never acted on.

Even with the plastic—which despite clean-up efforts did not diminish, since every high tide brought in more—the place remained beautiful and wild. It felt like something out of a romantic past that had vanished from most of the earth. I had visions of what it must have been like to embark on the beaches of North America for the first time only five centuries before: untouched, untarnished, undeveloped, stretching as far as the eye could see. If the tropical forest were replaced with deciduous, this could be 16th century Virginia.

After our walk we returned to our little room and feasted on beans and rice. We read and waited until a few hours after dark when we would join all of Warana's population on the long beach looking for nesting leatherbacks.

Finally, it was time. We checked our flashlights. We threw on long pants and laced up hiking shoes. We filled a backpack with more than we needed—water, hats, extra clothes, etc. (as the two weeks went by the backpack grew lighter until we stopped using it altogether). Then we met Liz and the others at the entrance of the lodge; from there we went down to the beach.

We walked quickly over the obfuscated beach with hardly a light on. My eyes attempted to focus on the sand beneath my feet, trying to make sure I didn't step on something untoward. I could make out the people around me, but they were just shapes, grayish blobs in the black. Coming from a world without true darkness, I felt blind.

Liz had forsaken lights altogether on these walks; although it was a cloudy night, she said her eyes adjusted quickly now and that the lack of light actually helped her see the enormous leatherback tracks (she turned out to be right). She had begun by seeing by the stars; now she saw by the ocean. My wife and I—not yet so celestially or pelagically inclined—carried flashlights with their heads wrapped in red cellophane, since the turtles were sensitive to any light but red.

We struggled to keep up, and every log and branch looked to me like something slithering and venomous. Of course, what I should also have remembered while following Liz at a breakneck pace was that it would be wholly unnatural to have a venomous forest snake out on the beach in the open—such serpents were content to hide themselves in the leaf litter or the sheltered corners of people's homes

Fortunately it wasn't ten minutes until we came upon our first leatherback turtle and all thoughts of jumpy snakes vanished. Everywhere red flashlights switched on, murmurs filtered through the small group, and my wife and I stood in awe as Liz, business-like, began her work.

Months of anticipation had not prepared us for this turtle. In fact this was one of those animals where years of study could not prepare one for an actual encounter. The marine turtles that one sees in pictures and on film are usually very turtle-like: a large round shell with flippers instead of legs. But the leatherback is more leviathan than turtle. It seems to have crawled out of a time machine from the Triassic.

In the gray darkness its massive flippers cut the sand and, with strength that could break a man's leg, tossed it away; its reptilian head moved up and down as the beast let out a low quiet groan. It was monstrous, terrible, and beautiful, like something out of Albrecht Durer's prints.

During the fourteen days we spent in Galibi, we saw well over twenty leatherbacks. Eventually, one becomes accustomed to such monsters, as humans have the startling ability to become accustomed to anything. But even in the last days, it would only take a moment— while we were scuttling around in the dark marking the leatherback's nest, measuring her carapace, or checking for tags—for us to recall starkly just how jaw-dropping the animal is.

The leatherback's deep evolutionary history is the reason for its singularity, both in appearance and behavior. The leatherback is the last surviving member of the family Dermochelyidae, which first appeared 110 million years ago during the Early Cretaceous. The species differs from other marine turtles in so many fundamental ways it is difficult to know where to begin. Unlike its somewhat close relatives, the leatherback does not possess a normal hard and bony shell; instead its carapace is covered by skin, leaving no space between shell and body. None of the marine turtles can pull their head and limbs under their shell like terrestrial turtles, but even if they could the leatherback would have no space to pull into: there is no gap. Easily the largest of the turtles, the leatherback retains even more extravagant titles: heaviest and fastest reptile on earth. A male leatherback stranded in Wales was weighed at a record of 2,020 lbs (about the size of a water buffalo or a very big polar bear). At its longest it can reach nearly seven feet.

Leatherback turtles not only look nothing like other marine turtles, their behavior is unique. Feeding almost exclusively on jellyfish, leatherbacks are deep divers. Actually, that is not strong enough: leatherbacks are abyssal divers, having been recorded diving as far down as 4,200 feet. In order to regulate their temperature while diving to colder and colder depths, the leatherback has evolved several adaptations: counter-current heat exchange, high oil content, and a large body size, all of which make their metabolic rate four times what would be expected in a reptile of their size. Leatherbacks not only dive nearly a mile down, they also travel the world. Migrating across oceans, these great reptiles see more of the world than the vast majority of humans: one leatherback was recorded as having swum twelve thousand miles in a year, from Indonesia to Oregon. They do this by cruising at a swift 22 miles per hour.

All of these facts and details cannot be recalled when you see one for the first time: all this is lost in awe.

Liz, however, was not overcome. Instead she was opening her bag, pen in her mouth, and taking out a measuring tape, string, and a scanner for tags. This is how we proceeded for two weeks: first we would measure the turtle from one end of the carapace to the other, careful not to step where the massive animal's flipper could catch us off guard and knock our legs out from under us; next we would scan the leatherback's flippers and head for tags, which other biologists, perhaps half-way across the world, might have placed just beneath the skin so it could be identified in a database; then, as the leatherback laid her eggs, we would insert a string into the nest and tie the other end of the string to a stick placed higher in the dunes, so the next day Liz could find the nest and, using markers, triangulate its position; once this was finished we moved on down the beach looking for our next target.

All of this occurred in darkness. Yet, about a week into our time at Galibi we were fortunate to have the rare opportunity to watch a leatherback lay her eggs during a broad and bright afternoon. We observed the turtle from the moment it rose out of the sea like some Greek deity until, maybe an hour later, it propelled itself with its massive flippers back into the surf and finally disappeared.

The leatherback's laying process is laborious. After freeing herself from the water and entering the alien world of the land, she uses her massive front flippers to propel herself, stroke by laborious stroke, up the beach. At some point she decides she has gone far enough—most often she is right, but once in awhile she lays her eggs below the tide line, dooming them from the beginning (in this case Liz would return the next day to dig up the nest and move it to a hatchery). And then she begins the long process of digging out her nest with her hind flippers. Once the nest is done she lays the eggs, usually just under a hundred. Lifting her head she groans softly and goo drips from her eyes. When she has laid her whole clutch she delicately covers the eggs with sand as only a mother can. Then she camouflages the nest. She does this by moving around in circles while her massive forelimbs toss up sand everywhere, so predators, including humans, have no idea where to start digging for the nutrient-rich eggs, since a few square meters of sand have been disturbed. Once she finishes camouflaging the nest, she makes her way back out to sea, disappearing beneath the surf. She will probably resurface a few more times to lay additional nests—as many as nine—before she forgoes the beach entirely and heads back to open ocean.

She will return every few years to lay again. Her lifespan has been said to be somewhere between forty and one hundred and fifty years—obviously no one knows for certain and, like an anaconda's maximum length, reports vary widely. Once a leatherback achieves adulthood it has no natural predators—except modern-day humans.

The same is not true of other marine turtles. Although we spent our time focused on the leatherback, Galibi is a nursery for several other sea turtles, including the green turtle, the olive ridley, and, rarely, the hawksbill. It was no longer the right time of the year for the olive ridleys or hawksbills, but green turtles would come up every night along with the leatherbacks. The greens, however, were easier to spook and since they were not a part of our project we gave them a wide berth. The green turtle looks rather diminutive after you've spent several nights working with leatherbacks. In laying eggs, the green turtle scurries past the leatherbacks into the dunes and shrubs—that strand of land between beach and forest. By choosing to lay its eggs there, it avoids the danger of a high tide drowning the clutch, but leaves itself open to another threat.

One night while we were there, a jaguar came onto the dunes, grabbed hold of a green turtle's head, crushed it, and employing its incredible strength pulled the giant turtle deeper into the brush. The next morning one of the guys, Bep, saw the jaguar flee into the forest. Following the trail he found the green's body. He showed us later in the day. It was headless—the head is what the jaguar eats first. In addition, one front flipper had been torn off. One could see inside the turtle itself through the gaping hole of its headlessness. Its back flippers splayed helplessly against the sand, denoting that it had in fact been dragged. The next morning the sea turtle disappeared altogether; the jaguar had pulled it into the forest, leaving a lone flipper where the sea-grazing herbivore had died. Greens are a weighty animal, reaching over 400 lbs, and even for a jaguar as big as 200 lbs it is incredible to think of this cat pulling the sea-shelled animal to its lair.

When a full-grown green turtle is killed by a jaguar, it provides additional food for black vultures, those ever-dependable sentries of the coastline, which perch on the tall jungle trees like sailors in a ship's yardarms. In addition, black clouds of flies appear around the corpse, and ants and maggots gorge themselves.

While the green turtle will feed multitudes, it's the infant turtles that feed the greatest variety of predators—both on land and sea. It is estimated that one in a thousand baby turtles survives long enough to reproduce. If this is at all accurate, it would take over ten nests to produce just one irrepressible James Johnson (of the Dunbar shipwreck). After a mother lays the nest, the undeveloped offspring become fair game for just about anything: ants, possums, ghost crabs, vultures, hawks, and humans. A hatched nest is even more vulnerable: the walk from eggshell to sea is probably the marine turtle's most perilous journey. One nest we found had been invaded by large red ants with massive mandibles; clinging to the newly-born turtles, these ants slowly wore out the juvenile reptile's resistance. Vultures will knock the infant on its back—easy to do to something so assailable—and peck into its underside. Once the turtles make it to sea and the sweet rhythmic surf, one would think they would be granted a reprieve, but from the moment they enter the water, they are in grave danger of predatory fish.

It is this collision between terrestrial and marine life in Galibi that makes it endlessly intriguing: one could hardly imagine more alien worlds meeting. But the turtles made up just one part of this transition environment, described by scientists as an 'ecotone'. There were myriad other players. During the long sun-satiated days, a troupe of squirrel monkeys kept us company as they routinely invaded a cashew fruit tree. Varied lizards sunned themselves in the daylight before creeping back into the jungle—or dark corners. One morning a tarantula had invaded the shower, making a shaving cup its home. Ants were so plentiful that I developed a calming ritual of scooping out dead ants from the boiling water whenever I added rice or pasta. One lazy afternoon, we watched a parade of ants carry a spider twenty times their size. Another day we found a massive dead fish being scoured by maggots. When the sun fell behind the forest, bats would cruise for insects and opossums emerge and scour the dunes of the beach, probably searching for infant turtles, fish, or crabs. One night, two of the marsupials stalked each other, hissing and screeching, on the upturned branch of a nine-foot cactus.

But in this world too, humans tip the balance. Historically, humans have sustainably hunted turtle eggs, using them as a protein-rich food source. Now the practice is illegal. The modern age has killed marine turtles so persistently—by pollution, artificial lights that confuse infant turtles, by-catch from commercial and artisanal fishing, and construction of hotels and resorts on nesting habitats— that egg hunting is now against the law almost everywhere, even in places where it provided indigenous groups with an important protein source. Commercial fishermen, however, can still catch turtles, drown them, and throw their old far-seeing bodies back into the sea with impunity. It is mostly a by-product of the fishing industry—and our pollution—that has caused every species of the marine turtle but one to become Critically Endangered. The leatherback is perhaps the most imperiled of all.

That first night we spent probably twenty minutes with the beautiful and awful female before moving on. Walking far more rapidly than I was comfortable with, it wasn't long before we reached one end of Liz's study site, an area covering about a mile and a half, and then turned around. We came upon a second leatherback and watched as Liz rapidly attained the information required; although we tried to help, at this early stage we mostly watched. Then it was back down the beach, senses heightened due to obfuscation and the undiminished pace. I again had the prescient notion of tripping on a log, stepping on a tropical spike of a downed tree, or stumbling onto something no one would ever want to stumble onto.

Suddenly out of the dark came the unexpected: an aggregation of Dutch. In a moment we were surrounded. The speakers were excited about something. They appeared to be trying to communicate with us; although they were so agitated they were all speaking at once. Liz pushed past the group like a native New Yorker pushes past tourists gawking at Times Square— and on down the beach we continued.

These Dutch were one-night tourists, out to see the turtles. They were staying in one of the villages downriver. They came often, Liz said. Few people in America had ever heard of Suriname, but Suriname is a major tourist destination for the Dutch. There is a simple explanation for this: Suriname was a colony of the Netherlands for more than three hundred years. Dutch is the official language, and just as many Americans love to travel to exotic places so long as the exotic peoples speak English, so also the Dutch prefer exotic places that speak their language.

I remember looking back once at the group, who had begun walking now in the opposite direction, their red-lit flashlights crisscrossing and moving rapidly in the night as though somehow signifying their amplified mood, before running on to catch up with Liz. When Liz walks, she walks. Exuding assurance as though she's heading up an army, she doesn't watch where she steps; she keeps her eyes ahead looking for the distinct markings in the sand that signify a turtle has come up recently. So my wife and I, finally getting into the rhythm, were thrown when suddenly she pulled up, stopped, and even took a few steps back.

The beam of a flashlight caught our eyes. We followed it to its subject and saw a large brownish snake, partially curled up. One of the guys from the lodge held the flashlight.

"Fer-de-lance," he said.

My pulse jumped and my stomach plunged.

"Poisonous," he added, as though his standing there with flashlight fixed on the meter-long snake required explanation. He may have just saved one of our lives. Quietly, he added that he had never seen this species on the beach before.

Nonetheless, here it was, the fer-de-lance—lingerer in my dreams for the last three months, symbol into which I poured all my anxiety about the month-long trip in general. In rational moments, I would tell myself: "the chances of you stumbling on a fer-de-lance are one in a…(add a seven digit number here)." But it was less than a meter from me now, swiveling through the sand, obviously agitated by all this attention.

Sometimes life is like this, even for a person prone to worry and obsessions: you waste untold hours worrying about some occurrence, you tell yourself how ridiculous and fruitless such concerns are, only to have it happen after all. Well, to be fair to fate, it didn't actually happen. I hadn't stepped on it and it hadn't sunk its teeth into my flesh injecting 200 milligrams of liquid toxin.

Responsible for the most snake bites in the region, the fer-de-lance has a tendency to bite before flight. Most snakes must be well aggravated in order to make a lunge with their fangs, but the fer-de-lance is the Billy Budd of the serpent world: it will lunge, mouth agape, head taut, and fangs spraying venom with the least provocation.

It was clear now what the Dutch had been excited about.

In the dark night on the beach, the snake appeared like a horror movie monster. In truth—and with some distance—it is worthy of great respect and admiration, and a certain understanding of the fact that when the snake bites it is not out of malice, but as protection from the world's most destructive species.

"Shit," Liz said. "We could have stepped right on it."

We could have, it's true. But we didn't, and now looking at it in the flashlight beam, watching its sinuous body twist and curl, seeing the pattern of yellow stripes, the scales like light-reflective chain mail, its well-shaped head and all-too-keen eyes, I couldn't help but notice how beautiful it was. How independent: to it we were an annoyance, an interruption in its hunt. Those glassy eyes didn't give a damn about our human self-importance, or our pats on the back for a planet well-conquered. Those eyes communicated something more to me. Despite all our supposed knowledge, our philosophies, our love of contemplating the divine, we would never know it. This legless night hunter would be forever beyond our comprehension, just as the leatherback resists description, and the headless anaconda's essence, even in death, could not be unraveled even by the species which split the atom, wrote Hamlet, and found a way to the moon. The trueness of life—even our own—still escapes us. We cannot be other than what we are, and therefore all we have accomplished has been merely exploratory—we remain ignorant.

What was the fer-de-lance doing on the beach? Was it hunting baby turtles like the black vulture or the ghost crab? Or was it—in my human-centric mind—merely trying to make me face my fears? The answer proved as hard to discover as why the anaconda was decapitated and left for dead. Six months and a lot of research later and I can't answer either question, not even superficially. I know this, however: in our short and often trivial lives, this would be one day to remember, to treasure, to turn over and over in my mind.

As we left the fer-de-lance to its own universe, I thought in my very human way not of its essence, but how it related to me, to my day. I did as humans have ever done: I made its appearance into a pattern; I constructed a story, a myth to explain the inherent mystery. It was a bookend, I decided. A fitting reflection of the beginning of our day: two snakes, one the largest in the world, but dead; the other, one of the world's deadliest and very much alive.

As the days in Galibi floated by and our fortnight dwindled, until finally we had to leave the wide beach, the unrelenting sun, the endless water, and the mysterious lives for the confines of white conference rooms, crowds of strangers, tea and coffee, computer and TV screens, I became increasingly aware of the strange, unheralded ecosystem we had left behind. I knew one thing: while I had no permanent place in such a world, I was happy to have been a sojourner there. While my understanding had not increased, my love of mystery had.

CITATIONS

:

Introduction: the life emergency

American Museum of Natural History. Biodiversity in the next millennium survey. 1998.

IUCN 2011. IUCN Red List of Threatened Species. Version 2011.1.

Murray A. Rudd. Scientists' Opinions on the Global Status and Management of Biological Diversity. Conservation

Biology, Wiley-Blackwell. 2011. DOI: 10.1111/j.1523-1739.2011.01772.x.

Meeting Tam in Borneo: our last chance to save the world's smallest rhino

Abdul Wahab Ahmad Zafir, Junai di Payne, Azlan Mohamed, Ching Fong Lau, Dionys i us Shankar Kumar Sharma, Raymond Alfred Amirtharaj Christy Williams, Senthival Nathan, Widodo S . Ramono and Gopalasamy Reuben Clements. Now or never: what will it take to save the Sumatran rhinoceros Dicerorhinus sumatrensis from extinction?. Oryx. 45(2), 225–233. 2011. doi:10.1017/S0030605310000864.

Will jellyfish take over the world?

Anthony J. Richardson, Andrew Bakun, Graeme C. Hays, and Mark J. Gibbons. The jellyfish joyride: causes, consequences and management responses to a more gelatinous future. Trends in Ecology and Evolution. Volume 24, Number 6. 2009

Why top predators matter

Robert L. Beschta and William J. Ripple. Large predators and trophic cascades in terrestrial ecosystems on the western United States. Biological Conservation. 2009.

Joseph K. Bump, Rolf O. Peterson, and John A. Vucetich.. Wolves modulate soil nutrient heterogeneity and foliar nitrogen by configuring the distribution of ungulate carcasses. Ecology. Vol 90, Issue 11. 2009

James A. Estes, John Terborgh, Justin S. Brashares, Mary E. Power, Joel Berger, William J. Bond, Stephen R. Carpenter, Timothy E. Essington, Robert D. Holt, Jeremy B. C. Jackson, Robert J. Marquis, Lauri Oksanen, Tarja Oksanen, Robert T. Paine, Ellen K. Pikitch, William J. Ripple, Stuart A. Sandin, Marten Scheffer, Thomas W. Schoener, Jonathan B. Shurin, Anthony R. E. Sinclair, Michael E. Soulé, Risto Virtanen, David A. Wardle. Trophic Downgrading of Planet Earth. Science. Volume 333. 15 July 2011.

Euan G. Ritchie and Christopher N. Johnson. Predator interactions, mesopredator release and biodiversity conservation. Ecology Letters. Volume 12, Issue 9. 2009.

The camera trap revolution: how a simple device is shaping research and conservation worldwide

Thomas E. Kucera and Reginald H. Barrett. A history of camera trapping. Pp. 9-26 in A. F. O'Connell, J. D. Nichols, and U. K. Karanth (eds.). Camera Traps in Animal Ecology: Methods and Analyses. Tokyo: Springer Inc. 2011.

Nature's greatest spectacle faces extinction

Cormack Gates and Keith Aune. 2008. Bison bison. In: IUCN 2011. IUCN Red List of Threatened Species. Version 2011.1.

Grant Harris, Simon Thirgood, J. Grant C. Hopcraft, Joris P. G. M. Cromsigt, Joel Berger. Global decline in aggregated migrations of large terrestrial mammals. Endangered Species Research 7:55-76. 2009. doi:10.3354/esr00173.

Patricia D. Moehlman, Nita Shah, and Claudia Feh. 2008. Equus hemionus. In: IUCN 2011. IUCN Red List of Threatened Species. Version 2011.1.

Joe Roman and Stephen R. Palumbi. Whales before whaling in the North Atlantic. Science 301:508-510. 2003.

David S. Wilcove and Martin Wikelski. Going, going, gone: Is animal migration disappearing? PLoS Biol 6(7): e188. 2008. doi:10.1371/journal.pbio.0060188

The penguin problem, or stop eating our fish!

Wayne Z. Trivelpiece, Jefferson T. Hinkea, Aileen K. Miller, Christian S. Reiss, Susan G. Trivelpiece, and George M. Watters. Variability in krill biomass links harvesting and climate warming to penguin population changes in Antarctica. PNAS, 2011. doi: 10.1073/pnas.1016560108.

What about the ugly ones?

Berta Martin-Lopez, Carlos Montes, and Javier Benayas. Economic Valuation of Biodiversity Conservation: the Meaning of Numbers. Conservation Biology, 2008.

Zoos: why a revolution is necessary to justify them

Hanson, Elizabeth. Animal Attractions: Nature on Display in American Zoos. Princeton University Press (January 26, 2004). 0691117705.

John H. Falk, Eric M. Reinhard, Cynthia L. Vernon, Kerry Bronnenkant, Joe E. Heimlich, Nora L. Deans. Why Zoos & Aquariums Matter: Assessing the Impact of a Visit to a Zoo or Aquarium. Association of Zoos & Aquariums. 2007.

The end of the oceans: from bounty to empty

American Chemical Society. "Hard plastics decompose in oceans, releasing endocrine disruptor BPA." ScienceDaily, 23 Mar. 2010.

American Chemical Society. "Plastics In Oceans Decompose, Release Hazardous Chemicals, Surprising New Study Says." ScienceDaily, 19 Aug. 2009.

Orea R. J. Anderson, Cleo J. Small, John P. Croxall, Euan K. Dunn, Benedict J. Sullivan, Oliver Yates, Andrew Black. Global seabird bycatch in longline fisheries. Endangered Species Research. 14:91-106. 2011.

Jeremy Jackson (2008). Ecological extinction and evolution in the brave new ocean. PNAS Online Early Edition for the week of August 11-15, 2008.

Mindy Selman, Zachary Sugg, Suzie Greenhalgh, Robert Diaz. Eutrophication and Hypoxia in Coastal Areas: A Global Assessment of the State of Knowledge. World Resources Institute. March 1, 2008.

Boris Worm, Edward B. Barbier, Nicola Beaumont, J. Emmett Duffy, Carl Folke, Benjamin S. Halpern, Jeremy B. C. Jackson, Heike K. Lotze, Fiorenza Micheli, Stephen R. Palumbi, Enric Sala, Kimberley A. Selkoe, John J. Stachowicz, Reg Watson.

Impacts of Biodiversity Loss on Ocean Ecosystem Services. Science 314: 787-760. 2006.

Saving the world's weirdest mammal

Samuel T. Turvey, Helen M.R. Meredith and R. Paul Scofield. Continued survival of Hispaniolan solenodon (Solenodon paradoxus) in Haiti. Oryx 42: 611-614. 2008.

Samuel T. Turvey and Sixto Incháustegui. 2008. Solenodon paradoxus. In: IUCN 2011. IUCN Red List of Threatened Species. Version 2011.2.

Shifting baselines: forgetting the lost

Sarah K. Papworth, J. Rist, Lauren Coad, and E.J. Milner-Gulland. Evidence for shifting baseline syndrome in conservation. Conservation Letters. 93–100. 2009.

Samuel T. Turvey, Leigh A Battett, Hao Yujiang, Zhang Xinqiao, Wang Xianyan, Huang Yagong, Zhou Kaiya, Tom Hart, and Wang Ding. Rapidly Shifting Baselines in Yangtze Fishing Communities and Local Memory of Extinct Species. Conservation Biology. 7th of January 2010. Doi: 10.1111/j.1523-1739.2009.01395.x

Gone: extinction over the past decade

J. Herrero and Jesús M. Pérez. 2008. Capra pyrenaica. In: IUCN 2011. IUCN Red List of Threatened Species. Version 2011.2.

Other mongabay.com books

RAINFORESTS by Rhett A. Butler

ISBN: 1463774575 / 9781463774578

An overview of tropical rainforests for kids, based on mongabay.com's popular web site for children (kids.mongabay. com). *Rainforests* describes tropical rainforests, why they are important, and what is happening to them. *Rainforests* is suitable for kids ages 10 and up as well as adults. Published September 2011

About the Author

Jeremy Leon Hance has been writing for mongabay.com since 2007. He graduated from Macalester College with a major in English and from St. John's College in Santa Fe with a Masters Degree in 'the Great Books'. He lives in St. Paul, Minnesota with his wife, Tiffany; his daughter, Aurelia; and his miniature Schnauzer, Oz.

Made in the USA
Charleston, SC
30 October 2012